MAN SEI!

MAN SEI!

The Making of a Korean American

by

Peter Hyun

A KOLOWALU BOOK

UNIVERSITY OF HAWAII PRESS

Honolulu

Manufactured in the United States of America

Library of Congress Cataloging-in-Publication Data

Hyun, Peter, 1906–
   Man sei!

   (Kolowalu book)
   1. Hyun, Peter, 1906–   . 2. Korean Americans—
Hawaii—Biography.   I.   Title.
DU624.7.K67H984   1986   996.9'004957   86–11314
ISBN 0–8248–1041–4

For Papa, Umma,
and the Hyun family,
and especially for
Luisa, my wife,
without whose untiring and
uncompromising editing
Man Sei! would not have
seen the light of day

A NOTE ON ROMANIZATION

For the spelling of Korean names and terms, I have followed what I call the old missionary system, which my father used throughout his memoirs, rather than the McCune-Reischauer system of romanization. There are a few exceptions, where I have followed the more familiar or commonly used spelling. For example, instead of *Lee* dynasty I have used *Yi*, which is the McCune-Reischauer system. Korean names are generally given with the surname first. For reasons unknown to me, my biblical name *Peter* was pronounced *Pedro;* similarly, *John* was *Johan,* *Joseph* was *Yosup,* and so on. My mother always addressed me as "Pedro-ya," the *ya* being like the Japanese honorific *san.*

CONTENTS

오늘 이렇게 조국지사의 영광 한날에
참석 하게 된것을 깊히 감사합니다.
머 국에 살고 잇는 우리형제 자매들은
함께 되어서, 결정 한것은 아버님과 어머님
의 유해는 그이의 조국강산으로 도라가서
그이의 동보들과 함께 있는 것이 맛당하고
깊은 것이라고 생각 헷음니다.
우리들을 길러 오실때에 가롯처 주신것은
이것임니다. "네들은 잇지마러라. 엇에서
살고 무슨 일을 하던지 네 나라를
사랑하고 네나라에 자유 독립을 위하야
생명을 밧처라." 이 밧은 사상은 아직도
잇지안코 사라갑니다.
아버님과 어머님은 우리동포 자유독립
을 위하야 로력 하시는것을 보고 자라 낫음니다.
그러나 아버님이 도라 가시기전에 원하시고
기도 하신것은 인민에 자유는 전세게 인생 성립
에 퍼지고 국가 독립은 세게 만국에 전부 광설
될것을 원하시며 기도하시면서 도라가 섯음니다.
또 다시 우리 어국지사을 위하야 이갓치 만히
노력을 하시고 이갓치 굉장하고 아름다운
묘지를 건설하여 주신것을 말할수 업는
깊흔 감상으로 감사 드림니다.

PREFACE

On August 8, 1975, the ashes of my father and my mother were interred in a grave on a hillside of the Korean National Cemetery in Seoul. In the midst of hundreds of their old friends and with the outpouring of tribute and honor as patriots and national heroes, they found their last resting place.

The interment was preceded by a solemn ceremony in the National Hall. A few surviving religious leaders, my father's contemporaries, as well as some high government officials eulogized Father's lifelong work for Korean independence.

In the presence of such venerable leaders and honored guests, I delivered my response. I had prepared the text the night before in Korean script. Its replica accompanies this preface. Any student of modern Korean language would recognize immediately that my style is old-fashioned, which is inevitable since my study of the Korean language ended when I was fifteen, more than sixty years ago. Nevertheless, I am grateful to have retained enough Korean to be able to express my thoughts and feelings in my mother tongue. Here is a translation of the text of my speech:

> Today, to be present on such a triumphant day for our patriots, I am indeed fortunate and deeply thankful. In America, my family of brothers and sisters met together and, after much debate, decided the following: The lifelong wishes of my father and my mother were to return to their motherland and be among their

own people. We agreed; returning their ashes to Korea would be a just and happy ending of their life.

While rearing us through the painful years of the Japanese colonial occupation, they taught us, "You must never forget. Wherever you live and whatever work you perform, remember and love your motherland and be prepared to offer your life for the independence and freedom of Korea." I have not forgotten these teachings.

I grew up watching my father and mother devoting all their energy in the struggle for national independence and the freedom of their people. My father believed freedom should spread among all peoples of the world and held independence to be the inviolable right of all nations. Such were his dreams and prayers before he died.

To you who have labored so valiantly to create such an impressive and beautiful National Cemetery as the final resting place for our patriots and national heroes, I offer my deep-felt thanks.

This moving occasion also gave birth to this book. Following the burial ceremony, my wife and I traveled by bus across the length of the peninsula, visiting Taegu, Kyongju, and Pusan. The countryside and the hills along the highway laced with winding rivers were incredibly green and beautiful. For me, this was a journey of discovery: discovery of ancient historical sites and the priceless remains of Korean culture. The stories I had heard in my childhood came to life now in a vivid context.

Visiting with people wherever we went, I met the new generation of Koreans. I found them full of life and confidence, but woefully ignorant of their heritage. Worst of all, they had hardly any knowledge of their recent history. They knew nothing of the Korean independence movement, of the struggle and sacrifice of thousands of Korean people to preserve the proud identity of Korea as an independent nation.

I felt personally responsible to tell the story of my father and my mother and their undying struggle for the freedom of their people. I had to tell the story as I had lived and witnessed it. Out of this conviction and inspiration *Man Sei!* was born.

INTRODUCTION

MAN SEI! MAN SEI! MAN SEI! Long Live Korea! Long Live Korea! For four thousand years, the rallying cry of the Koreans rang out across the mountains and down to the sea. Only once was it silenced. In 1910, it was forbidden by the Japanese during the time of their conquest and occupation of Korea.

Man Sei! is a particularly apt title for this book: the history of our family during those sad and dreadful times of cruelty and subjugation by Japan. And it is, first of all, the story of our father, the Reverend Soon Hyun. As one of the first Korean Christian ministers and longtime pastor of the famous Jung Dong First Methodist Church in Seoul, he led and inspired his people to seek their freedom—to once again shout *"Man Sei!"*

In 1919, Father with seven other patriots carefully plotted the great March First uprising against the Japanese colonial rule. And the Reverend Soon Hyun, in the guise of his calling, was the one chosen to cross the country from church to church organizing and alerting the people to the planned uprising.

On that day, March 1, 1919, hundreds of thousands of people took to the streets shouting *"Man Sei!"* and proclaiming their freedom. A Declaration of Independence was drawn up, signed by thirty-three leaders, and distributed throughout the country. After three days of stunned silence, the Japanese police and the military attacked and killed thousands of demonstrators; then all of the thirty-three leaders among thousands of others were arrested and imprisoned.

INTRODUCTION

Our father escaped with a price on his head. He evaded the Japanese police and fled to Shanghai, where he joined other patriots and exiles in establishing the Korean Provisional Government in Exile. Father was elected vice-minister of foreign affairs. That body in 1920 appointed Father ambassador plenipotentiary to the United States. He presented a formal petition to the then secretary of state, Charles Evans Hughes, requesting recognition and aid for the Korean Provisional Government. He traveled extensively, mobilizing the overseas Koreans in the United States, Hawaii, and the rest of the world.

One person in the United States who resented all of Father's activities was Syngman Rhee. He had lived in America all of his adult life and considered himself to be the sole Korean leader in the United States. Father's activities had damaged Rhee's prestige and pride, and by use of his well-known strong-arm methods he forced Father to abandon his efforts and return to Shanghai.

Following World War II, Father vowed never to return to a divided Korea, and he died in exile in Los Angeles in 1968. In August 1975, at the request of his people, his ashes with those of our mother, Maria Hyun, were returned to the land of his birth. There he was interred in the Korean National Cemetery in Seoul as a great patriot and national hero, surrounded and remembered by hundreds of people who had loved and admired him all these years.

And, too, *Man Sei!* is the story of our tiny, indomitable mother. Through much of her life she was left alone with her eight children while Father traveled around the country preaching and sustaining his people's hope for freedom. Singlehandedly, against all hazards and threats, including those of the Japanese police, she protected and reared her children. In 1920, she too escaped with her children—aged one to seventeen—traversed the Manchurian wilderness, crossed the landmass of China, and reunited the family with Father in Shanghai. Throughout the lean and unpredictable years in Shanghai, Mother held the family together and guided her eight children through all the perils of the Korean revolutionary movement.

Lastly, *Man Sei!* is my own story: my early childhood and adolescent years in Japanese-occupied Seoul. The daily insults and degradations I had to live with, though insufferable, were not as insidious as the precepts of Shinto-Samurai-Emperor worship I was forced to learn and recite and praise daily in school. I was a child of the 1919 uprising and a witness to the massacre of young students—boys and girls—by the Japanese in the Palace Square.

Taken to China by Mother, I joined the "Young Revolutionaries" —sons and daughters of the leaders—who dedicated their lives to the final victory of Korean independence. Our activities were filled with adventures, triumphs and failures, and, sometimes, tragedy. But the spirit of *Man Sei* always preserved and nurtured our courage.

The vicissitudes of the revolutionary movement once again forced us to a family exodus, this time from China to Hawaii. To me, the new world I was to discover was a part of America—a mysterious, magical land. I abandoned my second home, my "Young Revolutionary" comrades, and sailed across the Pacific with new foreboding but also new dreams.

1

MARCH FIRST

Man Sei! Man Sei! Man Sei!
Long Live Korea! Long Live Korea! Long Live Korea!
Dai-Han Dok Yip Man Sei!
Long Live Korean independence!

THE AWESOME CHANTS of the surging crowd still ring in my ears. It was Seoul, Korea, March 1, 1919; I was twelve years old. Countless thousands of Koreans—men and women, young and old, defying the Japanese police—poured out onto the streets of Seoul and, shouting and dancing, proclaimed their national independence. So once again, as their ancestors had done for four thousand years, the Korean people were putting an end to the rule of their conquerers—this time, the hated Japanese. For ten years, under the Japanese, we had suffered merciless oppression and humiliation. "Lazy Koreans!" "Stupid Koreans!" "Cowardly Koreans!" These were the epithets the Japanese hurled at us. To sweep away this national shame, the Koreans were now marching and shouting.

"*Man Sei! Man Sei! Man Sei!* Long Live Korea! Long Live Korea! Long Live Korea!"

"*Dai-Han Dok Yim Man Sei!* Long Live Korean Independence!"

The Japanese police were caught completely off guard. They stood by helplessly and watched the "meek Koreans" who, with their deafening cries, were shaking the very ground they were standing on. The long-repressed emotions of the people, unleashed at last, were piercing the air. Yet there was not even a hint of violence. As had been so carefully planned, the massive demonstration was disciplined and peaceful. This nonviolent uprising of the Korean people predated by many years the passive resistance movement of Gandhi in India. Korea is an ancient land; it boasts a history of over four thousand years. Koreans sing of their beautiful land:

> Three thousand *li* of mu-gung blossoms
> Clothe the beautiful mountains and rivers,
> Korea by the Koreans
> Shall be preserved forever.

Under the Japanese, of course, we were forbidden to sing this national anthem.

At the time of the March First uprising, our family consisted of my father and mother and eight children: four boys and four girls, ages one to fifteen. I was the oldest boy, followed by Paul, Joshua, and David. Sister Alice, the oldest one, was followed by Elizabeth, Soon-Ok, and baby Sister Mary. We were probably the first Korean family whose children, with the exception of Sister Soon-Ok, were given Western names. We also had traditional Korean names, but they were never used except by our relatives. My Korean name was Joon-Sup: "Flying Horse-Fire Flower." Besides, we didn't call our father and mother Abuji and Omuni as in customary Korean. Instead, we called them Papa and Umma, a variation of Western "Mama." Such was only one aspect of Father's personal crusade against feudal traditions and custom. This was not a small feat considering he was overturning a thousand-year-old family tradition.

The Hyun family traces its ancestors to Hyun Tark, one of the followers of Ki-Ja who came to Korea from China with scholars and artisans. He introduced Chinese culture to Korea and founded the kingdom of Chosun in the year 1122 B.C. The descendants of Hyun Tark spread over the northern province of Pyong-An. (Hyun is an uncommon Korean name which literally means "gray, as in the color of heaven.") According to the written record, the Hyun family was formally founded about the year A.D. 1130 during the reign of King Myung Chong of the Koryu dynasty. The founding father was a farmer named Hyun Dam-Yun. Together with his two sons, Dam-Yun formed an army of farmers, fought and defeated the forces of a traitor, and restored the king's crown. For his heroism, the king appointed Dam-Yun his "Tai Chang Kun" (Supreme Commander) and "Pyung Chang Sa" (Minister of War). Three hundred hectares of land were given to the Hyun family with all the rights of nobility in perpetuity. The Hyuns enjoyed these privileges until the fall of the Koryu dynasty in 1392. I learned of this proud family history from my grandfather and, later, from my father's memoirs.

Under the Yi dynasty which followed, the Hyun family lost its status of nobility and became "Jung-In," Middle People. The lowest class was known as "Sang-In," Common People. During the Yi dynasty, "Yang-Ban" or the Noblemen were mere figureheads in government; "Jung-In," the Middle People, did the work of running the government. In this period, the Hyun family became known as "Yuk-Kwan"—diplomats—and for eleven generations they held important positions in Sa Yuk Won, the Department of Diplomacy. Among them was Hyun Yil, my paternal great-grandfather, who was the personal advisor to Prince Tai Won-Kun, the regent to Kwang Mu, the last Korean king. This important office was later assumed by Yil's son, Hyun Chei-Sung, who was instrumental in introducing many new ideas in government—on agriculture, national defense, finance, and the selection of men for high office.

Hyun Chei-Sung, my great-uncle, was to distinguish himself when in 1866 a French naval expeditionary force attacked the fort guarding the capital and sailed up the Han River near Seoul. Hyun Chei-Sung was dispatched by the king to meet and negotiate with the French. He succeeded in persuading the French to withdraw and to establish friendly relations with Korea. Greatly impressed and appreciative of Chei-Sung's accomplishment, Prince Tai Won-Kun wished to restore the rank of nobility to the Hyun family, but Chei-Sung declined the offer. Such were the ancestral heritage and family traditions.

Now my father was attempting to guide his people and his family along a new path: the path of enlightenment as he perceived it in Christianity. The obstacles he faced were almost insurmountable. The opposition came not only from the old guard but from his own immediate family, particularly from his grandmother, the matriarch. It was

3

to her one day that a go-between brought a marriage proposal for Father, who was nine years old. The proposed bride was the grand-daughter of Princess Chin Hiun-Kim, the highly influential confidante of Queen Min. My great-grandmother, a wise matriarch, resisting the tempting riches and influence through such a marriage, rejected the proposal. A few years later when Father was old enough—twelve—she did select a bride for him: a fourteen-year-old daughter of Dr. Hai Chang Lee, the royal physician who looked after the king's family. Through a go-between, when all the negotiations were completed, they set the wedding date. In his memoirs, Father wrote about his wedding:

> It is rather embarrassing for me to tell about my marriage, but I want to tell you the truth. The bride was fourteen and I was twelve. After many minor dealings, the date for the wedding was set. So the little Miss Lee and the little Master Hyun were married under the sacred marriage rite on the tenth day of the eleventh moon [November] in 1890. The wedding took place in the bride's home in Mar-Chun County, about twenty miles to the north of Huang Dong [site of the Hyun's family estate]. I was in complete custody of my best man, servants, and maids. After per-forming some tedious ceremonies and tiresome feasts for three days, I was brought back home. This event took place chiefly for the honor and pleasure of my grandmother. The so-called Han Kap or the sixty-first birthday of my grandmother fell on the fourteenth day of the twelfth moon [December] 1890. The bride was brought to my home on my grandmother's birthday. There was a great feast at which about a thousand people were fed.

Out of such deep-rooted customs Father was striking out for a new, free world. He became one of the first Korean ordained Christian ministers, and for many years he was the pastor of Jung Dong First Methodist Church of Seoul. He then became the superintendent of Methodist Sunday Schools. In this capacity, he frequently traveled to all parts of the country. His missions were many and varied, but he was most famous for the religious revivals he conducted wherever he went. With his ringing voice and his fearless sermons, he would convert hun-dreds of people to Christianity at a single revival. His most compelling call was, quoting Jesus, "Follow me and I shall make you free." Koreans everywhere ached for their freedom. Even more than the attraction of education in the American missionary schools, it was this yearning for freedom that moved the people to flock to Christian churches.

It was only a fortnight before the March First uprising when Umma took all of us children, including Soon-Ok, my eleven-year-old invalid sister who had to be carried on the back of our caretaker to the South Gate railway station to see Papa off. But why? On those evangelical trips, the family had never gone to the station to see him off. Only Umma knew that Papa was one of the leaders of the uprising and was leaving on the most important mission of his life. The mission, as I was to learn much later, was to smuggle himself out of Korea to China and there to organize every possible diplomatic activity on behalf of Korean independence. Like his forefathers, Papa too had been appointed as chief of diplomacy by the leaders of the March First movement. His past role in the church would enable him to travel unnoticed by the Japanese police and reach China before the outbreak of the March First uprising. Even Papa didn't know then that he might never again set foot in his motherland.

We were brought up not to show our emotions, least of all in public. But before parting on that day, when Papa patted the heads of us older children and gently pinched the cheeks of the younger ones, I could almost feel his unshed tears. We all watched him as he stood before Umma and they looked at each other in a long silence. Other than that, Papa's departure was uneventful, except that at the last moment my younger brothers Joshua and David ran and clutched at Father's legs and held on. Startled, Papa scolded them affectionately: *"Ee-nom-ah! Ee-nom-ah!* Rascals! Rascals!" He quickly picked up his valise and walked to the gate where an attendant punched his ticket and let him through. I leaned against the railing and watched him climb the steps and disappear into the train.

So it was on the fateful day of March 1, 1919: Umma was left alone with her eight young children. With Papa gone, it was now up to her to feed and protect us. As days passed we grew more and more dependent on Umma as our provider, our arbiter, and our guardian. With the echoes of *"Man Sei! Man Sei!"* in the streets, Umma gave us

5

strict orders to remain indoors. For two days, from inside the house, I heard the roars and rumblings of the people on the street. I was excited but I did not quite understand the meaning of *"Man Sei."* In a hushed voice Umma explained it to me.

"Man Sei! Ten Thousand Years! Long Live Korea! Long Live Korean Independence! Pedro-ya, it means we are free. It means we are not Japanese slaves anymore." Listening to Umma, more than ever, I wished to go out and join the people in the street.

On the morning of the third day, my mind was made up, and at the first opportune moment, I dashed out of the house. I met a group of students who told me they were headed for the Chang Duk Palace Grounds; people of the whole city were to assemble there for a great independence celebration. In high excitement I followed the older students. I had passed the palace grounds often going to and from school. The main gate of the palace was so big and wide that at least ten men would have to stand in line with their arms extended to be able to span it. Two smaller gates flanked the center gate, and over them an immense tile roof gracefully spread its curved tips like giant wings. I had never seen the inside of the palace for the gates were always shut. There was a tiny opening in one of the smaller gates barely large enough for a person to pass through. In front of this opening, a uniformed soldier with a rifle on his shoulder slowly paced back and forth. Whenever I passed him, I would cast a surreptitious glance at his expressionless face and wonder if he could really repulse all intruders.

Walking along the palace wall prompted my companions to gossip in whispers about the king who lived in the palace. "The king was really an idiot," the older student hissed and added, "and he always wet his pants." We all laughed but we didn't believe him. He then went on seriously, "No wonder he lost his country to the Japanese! And worse, he even lost his only son. Do you know, the Japanese spirited the young prince away to Japan and forced him to marry a Japanese 'princess'!" Yes, most of us had heard the story but didn't know if it was really true.

"Listen!" The older student called for our attention. "They say she is not really a princess but a common woman." He finished the story with a sneer, "She wasn't even pretty to look at. . . ."

The crowd heading for the palace grounds was growing larger and we had to hurry our steps. Yet I kept remembering that special night when the whole family went to the railway station to bid farewell to Father. The famous South Gate Road had seemed especially brilliant and lively that night; all the shops were brightly lit and the vendors under kerosene lamps hawking their offerings seemed to be in high spirits. People milled about looking for bargains or just enjoying the evening stroll. I took deep breaths of the aroma of foods arising over the stalls: steaming bowls of noodles, hot rice cakes with sweet beans, meats and onion on skewers broiling over charcoal fires. But my favorite smell was the scent of roasting chestnuts and sweet potatoes. The picture of the vendors moving about in the flickering light of the kerosene lamps struck me as so romantic that I swore to myself someday I too would have a stall on the South Gate Road.

I was jolted out of my daydreaming by another boisterous group of students joining the march. Now we were passing through the familiar Jung Dong Road. There were many famous buildings along this road, among them the Jung Dong First Methodist Church where Father had preached for many years and in whose parish all of us eight children grew up. We also passed the flight of steps leading to a green gate behind which stood the Catholic church. I was taught to scorn the Catholics because they worshiped man-made idols, even though some of them were the image of Jesus. A little further away was the American Tennis Club. Whenever I passed here, I would stop and peek through the fence and watch the Americans playing the strange game. They seemed the happiest people on earth; men and women in white costumes, jumping about, leaping, and chasing a little white ball wielding woven clubs in their hands, always laughing and screaming. Yes, these were the Americans who had been blessed because they believed in Jesus. Why didn't someone tell us Koreans about Jesus sooner?

Another building always fascinated me. Across the street from the Tennis Club there stood an imposing three-story brick building with wide granite steps leading up to the front door. Although intensely curious, I had never dared to venture inside the building. But some of my friends, braver than I, did go in and discovered what was inside. It was filled with strange foods brought over from America and sold to the missionaries, their children, and other white foreigners. I was awestruck when the boys told me that those strange foods performed miracles. It was these foods, they told me, that made the Americans so tall, their skin so white, their eyes so blue, and their noses so big. We would laugh and dare each other to eat the American food and risk becoming funny-looking like the Americans.

A burst of laughter once again shook me out of my reverie. A group of young women from Ewha College was joining the march. The Ewha, established by American missionaries, had become the most famous women's school in Korea. Its fame stemmed not only from its modern teachings, which included English, but also from the beautiful girls gathered there from all parts of the country. The sight of these girls always delighted me; their fresh, bright faces, their unpredictable peals of laughter, their animated chattering, and, most of all, their unfathomable mystery never failed to stir and excite me. They all wore the traditional Korean dress: pleated, bell-shaped white skirt and short blouse of delicate color. Their long black hair was braided with a bright red ribbon tied in a bow at the end. When they walked briskly, as they were doing now, the little red bow bounced in rhythm.

But what really happened on March First and the next day while I was locked in the house? By prodding the older students, I was able to piece together the story of the earthshaking events. At noon on March First, the populace of Seoul gathered in the Pagoda Park at Chong-Ro Square, the business center of the city. Precisely at noon, a leader appeared on the bandstand and, raising his arms skyward, shouted the magic words which the people then echoed.

"*Man Sei! Man Sei! Man Sei!* Long Live Korea! Long Live Korea! Long Live Korea!"

"*Uri Nara Dok Yip Man Sei!* Long Live Korean Independence!"

Out of nowhere the forbidden Korean flags appeared over the heads of the crowd as they roared thunderous "*Man Sei! Man Sei! Man Sei!*" again and again and again.

The shouts of the people did not stop until another leader appeared at the rostrum and raised his hands for silence. The new leader held up a scroll, unrolled it, and began to read in a deep solemn voice: "The Declaration of Korean Independence. . . ."

The people exploded in a deafening roar. When the leader resumed reading, the powerful and eloquent words touched the very soul of everyone listening.

MARCH FIRST

"In the name of thirty million Koreans, and for the preservation of three thousand *li* of Korean mountains and rivers, the unalterable and inviolable national independence of Korea is hereby proclaimed to the world."

When the cries subsided, the leader recited the names of the thirty-three signators of the declaration. The final instruction of the leader was then delivered.

"Go to the four corners of the city and celebrate this historic day. But remember! Let no one spoil the gravity of this day nor our honor with any indignities or violence."

The throng poured out of the park and scattered in all directions, shouting and singing and gathering more people as they marched. Those were the roars and rumblings in the streets I heard while I was forced to remain indoors.

For two days the Japanese police were completely baffled. So thoroughly secret was the planning of the uprising that the police were totally unprepared to cope with the situation. They were dazed and paralyzed by the immensity of the movement which spread throughout the country like a forest fire. But by the third day they were ready; the police had received their orders, and the reinforcement of the feared Japanese mounted marines renewed their arrogance. On this fateful day, my companions and I finally arrived at the palace grounds and saw the vast space filled with a sea of people. It was an awesome sight; over the heads of the throng, thousands of Korean flags fluttered as the mass of people, mostly young students, sent up wave after wave of *"Man Sei! Man Sei! Man Sei!"* With each outburst, the ground trembled. We were packed so tightly it was impossible to move and even difficult to breathe. We simply swayed from side to side in a solid mass.

Then it happened. At the height of the celebration, I heard the bloodcurdling screams of the Japanese mounted marines. They stood high on their horses and charged out of an alley like a pack of infuriated animals. Frozen on the spot, I watched helplessly as the mad dogs galloped blindly into the mass of people, swinging their long sabers right and left, right and left. They were chopping down the people like they were overgrown weeds. Screams of the falling and the felled pierced the air. Then, suddenly, the marines reared their horses and charged in another direction, cutting yet another swath through the human mass. They kept repeating this maneuver as though determined to cut down every living Korean. I was swept by the tide of the frightened people and somehow reached the outer fringe. I ran for my life. In sheer panic, I kept running until I couldn't run any more. Finally I had to stop and catch my breath. Only then did I remember my companions and the pretty girls from Ewha College. Where could they be? Were they all dead? How many Koreans were slaughtered at the palace grounds? No one would ever know.

Exhausted and still trembling, I reached home after dark. Suddenly it dawned on me that I had disobeyed Umma and had left the house. What punishment would I have to face? Bracing myself for the worst, I entered the gate. I saw Umma dashing out of the room and running down to meet me in the courtyard. How strange! She wasn't even angry and she didn't question where I had been all day. Instead, she came close to me and stroked my hair.

"Pedro-ya, you must be very hungry," she said softly. When I finished eating, she asked gently, "Now tell me. What did you see?"

In the days that followed, I learned of other attacks by the Japanese police and the marines. No one was ever to discover how many Koreans were shot, butchered, and imprisoned. One of the most horrible massacres took place in the village of Soo-Won, a little hamlet not far from Seoul. The Japanese ordered the entire populace of the village to gather at their church for special instructions. When all the men, women, and children had entered the church, the Japanese shut and boarded the doors. They then set the church on fire. Anyone attempting to escape from the inferno was methodically shot down by the police and the soldiers. This was more than two decades before the world was to hear of Lidice, the little village in Czechoslovakia which was wiped out by the Nazis in 1942.

Yes, the people grew fearful, but the fire of freedom had been kindled and the Koreans refused to let it die. It seemed the whole country went underground and all Koreans became soldiers fighting for their freedom. Farmers carrying their produce to the market, vendors hawking their offerings on the street, traveling merchants, students and teachers, monks and preachers, the marriage broker—all joined the ranks and did their part. They carried underground messages, printed and distributed leaflets and newspapers, and, most daring of all, they collected money from the people and kept the independence movement alive.

One day, an elderly deacon of Jung Dong Church who used to help my father came to visit us. Out of the white canvas bag in which he carried Bibles and other church literature, he pulled out a miniature newspaper; its name was *Korean Independence News*. Soon afterward, as might have been expected, he was arrested, imprisoned, and tortured. Amazingly, he was one of the few "Independence Workers" to come out of the prison alive. But when I saw him again, I hardly recognized him; he was a shrunken, broken man.

2

THE KING'S
FUNERAL

THE LAST KING OF KOREA died in January 1919, two months before
the March First uprising. He was the Emperor Kwang Mu until the
Japanese conquest in 1910 when his title was reduced by the Japanese to
that of king. In his lifetime, the king had enjoyed little respect from his
people; they scorned him as a weak, vacillating ruler who finally sur-
rendered his country to their most hated enemy, the Japanese. But now
that he was dead, the whole country sank into deep mourning and a
strange silence settled over the city of Seoul. The familiar chants of the
stone carriers drifting down from the hillside quarry were heard no
more, the chatter of women engaged in domestic chores vanished, and
in the evening, the lively drumbeats and the gay songs of the *kee-sang*
(geisha) and the revelers too were gone. Even the children playing in
the streets were subdued and quiet.

Silence.

To the Koreans, the death of their king meant the passing of the
proudest centuries of their national history: the Silla, the Koryu, and
the Yi (Lee) dynasties which had spanned over twelve and a half centuries. Silla, the first unified kingdom, was founded in A.D. 668 and based
its capital at Kyongju in the south. Silla was constantly besieged by
attacks from China over the land in the north and by invasions from
Japan across the sea in the south. While repelling all the attacks, Silla

succeeded in developing Korean culture to a new height. Great advancement in arts and letters, architectural achievements in the construction of magnificent monasteries and temples, and the flowering crafts of gold, silver, and precious stones were only part of Silla's golden age.

In the old capital city of Kyongju, the granite tower built as an observatory in the early Silla period still stands as a monument to this time of stunning achievements. It was from this tower that the astronomers forecast seasonal changes and weather for the farmers.

The "Ice House," possibly the earliest man-made refrigeration system, was another Silla accomplishment. A huge chamber was dug deep in the ground and a network of narrow canals was built to crisscross its floor. By ingenious engineering, the river water was brought up to flow through the canals, and when the walls of the chamber were sealed and layers of dirt covered its strong roof, the refrigeration systems was ready. In the winter, blocks of ice were cut from the frozen river and then hauled and stored in the Ice House. The natural insulation of the earth and the constant flow of the river water kept the ice frozen until the following winter. Thus the nobles and the rich were provided with fruits and vegetables in the winter and chilled beverages and meats in the summer.

After the conquest, Japan had made concerted efforts to destroy all vestiges of Korean culture but failed, as many of the great monasteries and temples had been built in the inaccessible mountain precipices. In any case, the Japanese quickly learned that the monuments and relics of Korean culture were valuable assets as tourist attractions and as such a considerable source of profit.

One of the most famous of these temples of the Silla kingdom is the Pulguk-Sa temple. It is built at the foot of Toham Mountain not far from the capital city of Kyongju. It is one of the five most famous Korean temples in existence. Though the many wooden structures of the temple have been rebuilt many times, the imposing compound has stood at the site for fifteen centuries. The intricate stone foundations on which the majestic temple structures rest give indisputable evidence of the architectural and artistic achievements of the Silla kingdom.

At the top of Toham Mountain, there is a unique Buddhist shrine called Sokkuram. This revered temple is carved into a mountainside, forming a veritable man-made grotto. According to tradition, pilgrims had to climb the mountain at night so that they could watch the sunrise and Sokkuram temple coming into view and see, far below, the beautiful valley of Kyongju awakening in brilliant colors.

The entrance to this temple bears the traditional circular columns supporting the arched roof with its curved eaves and massive wooden gate. But once over the threshold, the pilgrim is startled to find a most unusual temple hall. Toward the rear of the center, on a massive stone pedestal carved in the shape of a lotus, sits a giant Buddha whose serenity and posture exude eternal peace. This towering figure as well as the entire temple hall and every embellishment in it has been cut and carved out of the granite mountain. Around the Buddha in a semicircle, the mountain walls have been chiseled in a row of tall panels, and in the panels, larger than life-size figures, the protectors and guardians of the Buddha are sculptured in relief. It is hard to believe that such beauty and grandeur were at one time only a formless mountain.

In its last century, this flourishing kingdom was torn by destructive internal strife. The triumph of the dominant faction under Wang-Keun led to the birth of a new kingdom called Koryu in A.D. 953. (Undoubtedly, the Western world adopted the name Korea from this period.) The capital was moved north to Songdo, or Kaesong as it is known today. The town of Panmunjon, where the truce of the Korean War of 1950–1953 is still being administered, is located near this old Koryu capital.

This newly found kingdom, too, faced ceaseless foreign attacks: the powerful Mongols from the north and the ever-covetous Japanese from the south. In A.D. 1231 the Mongols under Genghis Khan swept down the peninsula, overpowered the capital, and forced its rule on Koryu. This was the first time in its long history that Korea had come under foreign domination. In the reign of Kublai Khan, the Mongols made two attempts to conquer Japan: in A.D. 1273 and again in 1281. In both these futile undertakings, Koryu was forced to provide the Mongols with men and material. When the Mongols finally withdrew, the Koryu kingdom lay in waste.

The calamities did not, however, keep Koryu from yet another resurgence of its culture. It reshaped its form of government, introduced civil service examinations for its officials, and promoted public education of the young. The Buddhist religion reached its height under Koryu, and the monks played a decisive role in determining government policy. It was under the Koryu dynasty that the art of printing was developed, and it was Koryu artisans who perfected the celadon pottery which today graces museums throughout the world.

But the Koryu kingdom sealed its doom when its last king was persuaded by the Buddhist monks to embark upon an ambitious adventure: the invasion of China. At the time, the Ming dynasty of China, which had overthrown the Mongols, was at the peak of its power. Ignoring all counsel, Koryu soldiers were ordered to march toward Manchuria, but when they reached the shores of the Yalu River they revolted against the suicidal march. The rebellion was led by General Lee Sung-Gae. He led his troops back to the capital, banished the monks, and forced the king to abdicate. The year was 1392; a new Korean dynasty, and the last, was born. General Lee, crowned as the founding king of the Yi dynasty, moved the capital to Seoul, and to guard it a massive wall was built around the new city. All Buddhist influence on the government was eliminated by banishing the priests and monks to the mountains, and their land was seized and distributed to the farmers.

But Korea under any rule was not to be left free from attack. In 1592, Japan staged an all-out campaign to consummate its age-old dream. The Japanese warlord, Hideyoshi, with a 250,000-man force, launched a massive attack, and the ill-equipped and ill-trained Korean soldiers retreated to the north. For seven long years the Koreans fought off defeat. The Yi kingdom faced the prospect of complete ruin but for the great feat of Admiral Lee Soon-Shin, Korea's most renowned patriot. He invented the "Turtle Ship," the first armored warship in history. With these Turtle Ships, Admiral Lee attacked and sank most of the Japanese fleet, and he put the rest to flight. Hideyoshi was forced to abandon his dream and withdraw in defeat. But the Yi kingdom hardly had time to recover from the devastation of long years of war when it was invaded again. This time it was the Manchus who had overthrown the Ming empire. Fortunately, the Manchus were satisfied with the capture of some hundreds of Koreans as slaves and withdrew.

Despite incessant attacks from the outside, the Yi kingdom managed to push ahead with its cultural advances. The greatest single achievement was the development of the Korean phonetic alphabet, unique and perfectly suited to the Korean language. The Koreans owe their high rate of literacy to the alphabet. The Yi dynasty also produced movable type fifty years before Gutenberg of Germany. In the ensuing upsurge of the printed word, the Korean encyclopedia and many great works of literature were published. Old Buddhist temples were turned into schools. Learning was honored and encouraged, and the teacher was accorded the highest rank in society. But Korea was weary of the outside world; all national doors were shut and all contacts cut off. Korea became known as the "Hermit Kingdom."

When in 1853 Commodore Perry and the U.S. gunboats forced open Japan's door for trade, he inadvertently opened a new chapter of history for all Asia. Japan seized the opportunity to acquire modern weapons of warfare and, under Emperor Meiji, built a formidable modern army. Its immediate use, of course, was to be for the conquest of Korea. But first, Japan had to remove China from its path. This was accomplished easily by crushing China in the Sino-Japanese war of 1894–1895. The avowed purpose of the war, Japan declared, was to "protect Korea's independence."

But there still was another obstacle: the ominous shadow of the Russian bear. Czarist Russia, too, had long dreamed of securing Korea as a base of expansion to the Pacific. To meet the challenge, Japan proceeded to build a modern navy. She patiently spent ten years getting ready, and in 1904 declared war on Russia—once again, "to guard Korea's independence." Russia was then a great world power and Japan was given little chance against the colossus, but Japan startled the world by sinking the Russian fleet and forcing upon her a humiliating peace treaty. Signed at Portsmouth, New Hampshire, the treaty proclaimed, among other things, "the inviolability of Korean Independence." In desperation, the Korean king invoked the Mutual Aid Treaty of 1882 with the United States and appealed for help. President Theodore Roosevelt's response to the appeal was stern advice to the Koreans: "Cooperate with the Japanse." After a short period of sham maneuvers and intrigue, Japan finally discarded all pretext and formally annexed Korea in 1910.

How did it happen? Where were all the brave and proud Korean men and women? Where were the patriots and the heroes who had fought off all the invaders for thousands of years? Subjugation by Japan was the price Korea had to pay for its self-imposed isolation, for its refusal to face the emerging twentieth-century world. Korea had become a "Hermit Kingdom" just when Japan was mastering the Western technique of warfare. And the final curtain fell on Korea's proud history when its last king died, a prisoner in his own palace. Japan, the conquerer, magnanimously allowed the surviving members of the court to conduct a traditional royal funeral for the dead king: the last funeral ceremonies for the last king of Korea.

The city of Seoul swelled with people converging from all parts of the country and from all walks of life. The woodsmen from remote mountains and hills who gathered firewood for the country, the masons and the carpenters who built the mud-brick and thatched-roof houses, the paper hangers and the cabinetmakers who made oiled parchment and brass-hinged furniture for Korean homes, the artisans whose delicate hands fashioned beautiful ornaments of silver, gold, and precious stones—all the producers of Korea's wealth dropped their tools and came to Seoul for the king's funeral. Painters and calligraphers, too, left their brushes; priests and monks turned away from their pulpits and temples; teachers and students left their schools, colleges, and seminaries. All came to Seoul to bear witness to the burial of Korea's last king. They came by train, in horse and ox-driven carts, and on bicycles. But thousands of men and women simply walked. Women carrying bundles on their heads and men with bundles on their backs, the silent figures lined the country roads leading to the capital.

The throng of people converging on Seoul, besides their nondescript bundles, carried with them a deadly secret: the plot to use the occasion of the king's funeral for a nationwide uprising against Japanese rule. My father, traveling throughout the country as a Christian minister, was one of the carriers of the message of the planned revolt. That they could keep the secret from the Japanese police and spies until the outbreak on March 1 is a testimonial of the patriotism and unity of the Korean people at the time.

Even as a twelve-year-old, I could easily tell the visitors to the city. We children would point and call them "Sigul-Dugee"—country bumpkins. They didn't walk like the city dwellers; they moved not briskly but in slow measured steps. They also seemed lost; their eyes wandered here and there and they gawked at all the store windows. But the easiest country bumpkins to spot were the farmers. They wore poor and ill-fitting clothes and straw sandals. Their only apparent luxuries were the long bamboo pipes protruding from pantaloons and the tobacco pouches dangling from their belts.

They were humble in their manners and when they spoke their country accent sounded strange and comical. But still their appearance carried great strength and pride. Throughout Korean history, the farmers toiled and provided the country with its basic food: rice. To cultivate rice, the farmer had to bring water to the fields—by canals and ditches, by man-driven waterwheels, and by buckets on a pole carried across his shoulders. He had to tear open the hills and the mountains, build stone terraces, and fill the patchwork with water. On the high ground where water was too scarce and too meager to raise rice, the farmer planted wheat, barley, and beans as well as the Korean staple vegetables: cabbage, turnip, chili, lettuce, and cucumber. The sight of green hills throughout the whole peninsula is indeed a tribute to the work of the Korean farmer.

To this day, rice is often used as a measurement of wealth. Thousand-bushel family, five thousand-bushel family, ten thousand-bushel family, and so on refer to the amount of rice harvested from the land a family owns. I remember the elders of our family discussing the annual harvest from our family estate: forty thousand and fifty thousand bushels. In Korea, as in most Asian countries, the word to eat is literally "EATRICE."

At last, it was the day of the king's funeral. I got up early and put on my "New Year" clothes: white cotton pantaloons, white shirt and blue silk vest, and over them a long white tunic held together by wide blue ribbons tied in an elegant bow. I ate my breakfast hurriedly, all the while watching Umma with fear lest she might stop me from going to the funeral. Strange! She didn't question me, and before I finished, she got up and disappeared. I was free to leave the house and be on my way to the funeral. But I didn't dare go to the Chang Duk Palace Grounds where the funeral procession was to start; it would be so crowded, I wouldn't even be able to get a glimpse.

I got on the trolleycar at West Gate Road and took the long ride to Jong-Ro, the Bell Road in the center of the city. The street was so named for the huge "Independence Bell" which was housed in a little temple at the street corner. I was too late; the wide streets were already packed on both sides with people. Fortunately, I had enough pennies left in my pouch to ride the trolleycar once more and head for the East Gate, the end of the city. But it was hopeless! Here too a dense crowd was milling about and jostling for vantage points. I walked around the gate and along the country road which eventually would lead to the king's burial site.

Finally the crowd grew sparse and I found a space at the very front along the roadside. Standing and sometimes squatting, I began the long vigil for the funeral procession. I dared not move for fear of losing my excellent position, but overcome, and with tired legs, I finally sat down on the ground for a rest. I amused myself listening to the lively conversation around me.

"Oh, poor king! What a sad end!"

"Poor king? It was all his own fault. . . . He deserved his fate."

"Don't mock the dead, my friend. The king did his best."

"Yes, I know . . . his best! He let them murder his queen, kidnap his son, and then surrender his country to the enemy . . . his best!"

"It's too late for anything now. Just the same, what a sad day. . . ."

"You know, I have never seen a king's funeral."

"Well, thanks to your King Kwang Mu . . . you'll see one today."

There was a brief lull, and then another group picked up the conversation.

"Don't be bitter, my friends. What could he have done?"

"Killed himself, if he had any pride."

"What good would that have been—except more jeers from the Japanese?"

"It might have aroused the people to fight."

"Fight? With what? With flyswats and broomsticks?"

"Now, my friends, you are all filling the air with empty words."

"That's right. Confucius said, 'A saintly man does not stain his hands with blood.' "

"Confucius never knew the Japanese. . . . They would gladly swim in blood to conquer our country."

The conversation was growing more heated; after a moment of silence, someone admonished the others.

"Not so loud, my friends. . . . You know, the Japanese have ears everywhere."

CHAPTER 2

"Let them listen! Let them hear all they can!"

"Poor king! After five hundred years of proud reign. . . . What a disgraceful end for the Lee kingdom. . . ."

"Don't forget the Japanese have been waiting for over a thousand years."

Abruptly all conversation stopped and a wave of murmurs arose from the crowd. In the distance, we could hear the wailing sound of the *piri*. The *piri*, one of the oldest Korean instruments, has a foot-long metal tube flaring at the end like a funnel. A bamboo-reed mouthpiece is affixed at the opposite end through which the musician blows and fingers the holes in the stem, producing a pure and piercing sound of varying pitch and intensity. At last the royal procession came into view and the people stirred in excitement. First came the formation of musicians wearing colorful court costumes and jaunty high hats. The ear-shattering mournful cry of the *piri* was accentuated by the regal strut of the musicians.

Behind them came the drummers. The *jang-gu,* the age-old Korean drum, resembled two large bells whose necks were ingeniously tied together in the center, the wide ends covered tightly with fine animal skin. A silk band is tied to the drum and slung across the drummer's shoulders, leaving both his hands free to play it. Using the palm and fingers of his left hand, he beats out the dominant rhythm, and with a thin, flexible bamboo stick in his right hand he beats out the titillating syncopation. The *jang-gu* and Korean dances are inseparable; whenever the beat of the *jang-gu* is heard, people move their feet and sway their bodies.

More musicians followed, some with strange instruments I had never seen before. I easily recognized the flutes and, as always, was fascinated by their ethereal sound. There were flutes of many sizes and styles, some blown vertically and others horizontally. The assembly of flutes playing together was deeply pleasurable and moving. Formations of other musicians passed by, including some playing long trumpets and giant brass cymbals. At the end came a row of great temple drums. Each drum was tied to a pole, carried by two men. The master drummer followed behind holding a big drumstick in each hand. With majestic movements he beat the drum whose reverberating rumbles passed over the procession.

Now came a forest of banners fluttering from the tops of long bamboo poles being carried by men in colorful costumes and the traditional tall hats. On the multicolored banners—white, yellow, blue, lavender, and vermilion—there were writings in heroic letters. Except for a few characters, I didn't understand all the words; I only surmised that they were words of eulogy for the dead king. After the banners came the parade carrying the king's most intimate personal effects, the parade of parting gifts from his loyal servants, and a special group carrying gifts to the king's ancestors. The long line of urns, vessels, bowls, and chests of many sizes and shapes were borne by the court carriers wearing dazzling costumes. All the gifts, I was told, would be buried with the king in the tomb. What a pity, I thought, to bury all the priceless treasures.

Now came brilliant white streamers whose carriers, too, were in white costume and white high hats. The pure white steamers were cleansing the path for the approaching "Little Bier." It was so called because the coffin in the Little Bier did not carry the body of the dead king. In the olden days, the coffin would be carrying the body of the king's favorite servant to accompany the king and serve him in the other world. Today, the second coffin was being carried only as a symbol. The Little Bier was built in the shape of the King's Chamber with four circular columns supporting the winged roof. The sides of the chamber were left open so that the empty coffin resting in the center could be viewed from all sides.

The Little Bier was raised on a wide platform under which an intricate system of supports and rows of bars enabled some fifty bearers to lift and carry the structure on their shoulders. Its weight must have been great, but the bearers in white costume and hats moved in unison in graceful steps. They swayed from side to side to the accompaniment of their mournful chant:

> *Yongchigi Yongcha!*
> *Yongcha! Yongcha!*
> Lift high! Lift high!
> Lift! Lift!
> *Yongchigi Yongcha!*
> *Yongcha! Yongcha!*
> Lift high! Lift high!
> Lift! Lift!

The beautiful Little Bier moved away slowly. The elders explained that the Little Bier would be entombed in front of the Grand Tomb where the king's body would be laid to rest. I was delighted; I had never seen such royal pomp and such enchanting royal costumes. The Japanese had forbidden even the showing of any pictures of Korea's historical past.

Once again I heard the shrill cry of the *piri,* leading another contingent of musicians. Every group in this contingent seemed more impressive, and their music rose over the whole procession with grandeur, transporting the people into another world. Soon the Grand Bier came into view and its splendor overwhelmed everyone. It was a replica of the "Floating Palace," the king's favorite playland. Built entirely of solid granite, the palace itself rested in the middle of a lake filled with lotus. The pavilion had no walls; only the slender stone columns held up the gracefully curved roof. From the shore, people could see the shaded interior and could almost smell the sweet scent of lotus blossoms floating through the immense hall. On warm summer evenings, the king and his retinue would come to this Floating Palace to revel. There they would drink rice spirits and nibble on rare delicacies while composing and reciting poetry. They would then sing and slap their thighs loudly to the rhythm of the musicians and the dancers.

Now, this miniature replica of the pavilion was carrying the body of the dead king. A hundred men in white costume and white high hats were carrying the enormous structure on their shoulders. But without any visible strain, the bearers moved in graceful steps and raised their voices in a mighty chant:

> *Yongchigi Yongcha!*
> *Yongcha! Yongcha!*
> *Yongchigi Yongcha!*
> *Yongcha! Yongcha!*

The Grand Bier swerved and teetered precariously and the people gasped. Unconcerned, the bearers moved on with dancing steps. Every now and then a new bearer would dash over and relieve another without missing a step or interrupting the rhythmic movement.

I could see the imposing coffin in the center of the bier. Why was the coffin so big? I wondered. Of course, they must have placed every conceivable article in it that the king might need for his long journey to meet his ancestors: robes and gowns for all seasons and occasions, vessels of rice wine and his favorite porcelain cups, and inkstone, brushes, and rolls of fine rice paper, a flute or two for his amusement, and most certainly his royal seal in a golden box. Of course, the king's coffin had to be enormous.

There followed behind the Grand Bier a retinue of men in long-forgotten uniforms. They were following the bier on foot with their heads bowed. These were the officials favored by the Japanese and allowed to remain in the king's court. They shuffled along in silence, ashamed or afraid to raise their heads and look at the people. The funeral procession was quickly coming to an end.

Suddenly, a heartrending wail shot out of the crowd.

"Aigo! Aigo! Aigo!"

"Aigo! Aigo!"

It was the traditional wailing that had been heard throughout Korean history whenever there was a funeral; it was a cry of mourning, farewell, and prayer. Its tragic tone had become ingrained in the voice of the Korean, and the quality of sadness could be detected in his speech and songs.

"Aigo! Aigo! Aigo!"

The wails soaring, people dashed out and joined the procession. The haunting cry swelled as though they were beckoning the king to come back. But the king in his Grand Bier was fast disappearing, leaving in its wake only the swirling dust and the faint cry of the *piri.*

I turned away from the crowd and started the long walk home. Suddenly I felt spent and hungry and a very strange feeling came over me; I had just witnessed a river of tears emptying out of a whole people, out of a whole country. I had no more money but I jumped on a moving trolleycar already bulging with people. Nobody seemed to care, least of all the conductor who wasn't collecting fares from anyone. It was dark when I arrived home.

"Pedro-ya!" Umma rushed out to greet me at the gate.

"You are so late, Pedro-ya. . . ."

"Yes, Umma, I know."

"You must be starving. . . . Did you have anything to eat?"

"No, Umma," I said, "but I'm not hungry." I was surprised to hear myself saying that when I hadn't eaten anything all day and I was famished.

"Come on in." Umma held my hand and led me into the room. "Sit down here . . . I'll bring something to eat right away." This was the main room in the house; we ate all our meals here, and at night we spread our mattresses and all slept in the same room. Baby Sister Mary was already asleep, but the rest of my brothers and sisters gathered around me to hear about my adventure. Big Sister Alice asked me if the people at the funeral were really sad, and Sister Soon-Ok, the dear crippled one, asked about the royal costumes, but the rest just stared and waited for me to tell my story.

Since Papa's departure, I noticed that Umma was treating me more and more like the man of the house. She was now carrying in the little lacquer table which used to be Papa's dining table. She set it before me and said, "Here is your supper, Pedro-ya. . . . Hurry and eat." The little table was laden with a sumptuous meal, and I could see my brothers and sisters staring with envy. The "supper" was really a festive dinner: a steaming bowl of rice, a large bowl of my favorite beef-bone soup, bean sprouts and radish salad, and a dish of sizzling *bul-go-gee,* marinated beef slices broiled over a charcoal fire. It was almost like my birthday or New Year's feast. But I couldn't really enjoy the dinner; the scenes of the funeral procession and the disturbing words of the people surrounding me still lingered in my mind.

"Here, Pedro-ya!" Umma shook me out of my dreaming. "Eat Pedro-ya. . . . Eat this delicious *bul-go-gee.* . . ."

"I'm too full, Umma," and I pushed the table to my brothers and sisters who gratefully ate all that remained on the table.

"Now, tell us," Umma said, "how many people were there at the king's funeral?"

"Oh, thousands, Umma, thousands. From Chang Duk Palace, Jong-Ro, and all the way to the East Gate, the streets were packed with people."

"So, they gave the king a good funeral, did they?"

"Yes, Umma, it was a very good one, especially for a king who had disgraced himself." Umma's eyes became blurred with tears. She asked no more questions.

3

CHILDHOOD

MY CHILDHOOD YEARS were short and passed swiftly, for they were spent in the most turbulent times of Korean history. Five hundred years of the Yi dynasty were coming to an end and Korea was struggling for its very life as an independent nation. The country was torn by internal dissension between the diehard royalists and the impatient reformists; between the advocates of capitulation and the uncompromising young radicals.

The Independence Club founded by Dr. Phillip Jaisohn, an American-educated Korean patriot, was the center of young progressives clamoring for reform and resistance to foreign encroachment. My paternal grandfather, who had served as governor under Emperor Kwang Mu, joined the club and began publishing a newspaper which gained considerable respect and popularity. My father, too, joined the club and became an ardent follower of Dr. Jaisohn. Among the junior members, there was also a young man named Syngman Rhee.

Alarmed by the growing influence of the Independence Club, the Japanese prevailed upon the vacillating king to force Dr. Jaisohn's return to America. Soon afterward, the club was nearly decimated by wholesale arrests of all its leaders, my grandfather among them. He spent several years in prison and then was sentenced to death. My grandmother confided to me that all of the family fortune was used as a bribe to secure his freedom.

My father had decided that modern education was the only instrument he could use to help his tottering country, but there was no such school in Korea. Thus his determination carried him to the land of his enemy, Japan. He enrolled in a college called Jun Den Kiu Ko Sa; the year was 1899. He plunged into the study of the twentieth-century view of the world: world history and geography and the emerging sciences of chemistry, physics, and mathematics. It was in this period that he also became exposed to Christianity. He began studying the Bible and attending church services. In 1901 he was baptized by a Baptist missionary, the Reverend Fisher. Of his conversion to Christianity, my father wrote: "Confucius teaches ethics, morals, and government; Buddhism teaches about three lives—former, present, and future life; Christianity teaches eternal life."

After graduation from college in 1902, he wished to continue his study in science, but for lack of financial means he returned home to Korea. He found the political situation had worsened, and under the pressure from the Japanese, Emperor Kwang Mu was suppressing and persecuting all who resisted the increasing Japanese domination. Even with his modern education, Father was unable to find any significant work. By chance, in response to a newspaper advertisement, he came in contact with the East-West Development Company, which was recruiting Korean laborers for the Hawaiian sugar plantations. Father accepted the position offered him as an overseer and interpreter for the Korean immigrants to Hawaii. His young wife, my mother, agreed to travel with him.

During his student years in Japan, she had managed all the household affairs for her parents-in-law. She weathered the death of Father's mother and that of his only brother, the imprisonment of his father, and the subsequent loss of family fortune. In the absence of Father, she managed through all the family crises and survived. When Father returned home from Japan, he and my mother had not yet come of age according to tradition and hadn't yet fulfilled their union as husband and wife. Now, at last, they were sailing in a foreign ship with a group of immigrant laborers bound for unknown shores. What a strange honeymoon! We children often asked Umma what Father looked like when she married him. She would giggle like a little girl and tell us, "Oh, he was so ugly!" But judging by the early photographs we found of him, we thought he was very handsome and dignified.

CHILDHOOD

Father and Mother arrived in Honolulu in February 1903; they were one of only five married couples among the one hundred and twenty Korean immigrants. Immediately upon arrival, they were taken to a sugar plantation and ordered to report for work the very next day. They worked ten hours a day, six days a week, and each received sixteen dollars a month. Father, as an overseer and interpreter, received thirty dollars a month. While looking after all the needs of the immigrant workers, Father organized a "Self-Rule Association" to help preserve their cultural identity as Koreans. In the evening, after work, he conducted classes in English for the workers. The news of his activities attracted many Korean laborers from other areas, and soon the Methodist Church in Honolulu invited Father to work for them.

He formally joined the Methodist Church and was assigned to look after all the Korean churches in the outlying areas. Now his family grew with the birth of his second daughter, Sister Elizabeth, in Honolulu. Big Sister Alice had been born on the sugar plantation of Waipahu the year before. In recognition of his leadership, the Methodist Mission appointed Father to be the preacher for all the Koreans on the island of Kauai, the "Garden Island." There, traveling on horseback, he covered the island from one end to the other, taking care of the sick, arranging schooling for the children, and conducting religious services. His sermons never failed to combine Christian faith with Korean aspirations for national freedom. Recognizing his value, some of the plantation owners began making regular financial contributions. Among them, the Wilcoxes and the Isenbergs became not only staunch supporters but also lifetime friends. With their help, Father built the first Korean church on Kauai; it was situated on top of a hill near the town of Lihue. Directly below this landmark was a beautiful little valley called Kapaia where, some time later, a two-story wooden building was erected as the parsonage for the traveling preacher. It was to this bucolic retreat, many years later, that Father was to return once again with his family of seven children.

At the moment, however, life for Father and Umma and their two daughters on the Garden Island was a constant struggle, and Umma was obliged to sew and mend the field workers' clothes to supplement Father's meager salary. Nevertheless, they were both rewarded by the growing consciousness and unity of the Korean community on the island, which was very appreciative and came to rely on Father and Umma for guidance and help. Another cheerful event at this time was the birth of their first son, me, the first Korean baby boy to be born on Kauai. Not only the Hyun family but the Koreans of the whole island were delighted with the event. At the time of my birth, Father was away from home on his usual tour of the island. Left alone, Umma gave birth with the help of a midwife, and the next day Umma went to the nearby stream to do the washing and cook the traditional seaweed soup for herself.

The news from Korea, meanwhile, grew more and more alarming: Japan was now dictating the forms and the policies for the Korean government to follow. A Methodist bishop whom Father had met at a church conference advised Father to return to Korea where he could serve more people. The bishop also assured Father of a position should he return to Korea. It was not easy for Father to abandon all the Korean laborers who had depended on him to look after them. But in May of 1907, Father and Umma took their three young children and sailed back to Korea; I was nine months old.

Father was met with a warm welcome from the religious and educational leaders, and in September of the same year he assumed the position of headmaster at a middle school in Seoul called Pai-Jai Hak Dang —"Cultural Hall of Learning." It was then, and still is today, one of the most famous educational institutions in Korea founded by the Methodist Mission. Besides English, Father taught many subjects such as world history, science, and mathematics. He also started a night school for the underprivileged, and on Sundays he preached regularly at the Seoul Central YMCA. He was invited to preach at various other churches including the famous Jung Dong First Methodist Church. His sermons were always inspirational, and thousands of people from throughout the city would come to hear him. Such gratifying response to his preaching led him to evangelical work. He toured the Korean communities in Manchuria and then throughout Korea conducting "revivals" in every village, town, and city. Countless thousands of people were converted to Christianity and Father became known as the Billy Sunday of Korea.

Those were turbulent days in Korea and my family, along with all the others, was tossed about like a lost ship in a stormy sea. Nonethe-

CHILDHOOD

less, there were memorable times and precious moments of my childhood years which I have treasured all my life. One such moment I remember was my first day in school. I was not quite six and considered too young for school. But I could not wait; I decided to follow my father to Gong-Ok Hak Kyo—"Bright Jade Learning Hall"—of which Father was the principal. Early one morning, I got dressed and hid outside, waiting for Father to leave for school in his rickshaw. When he appeared and got on and the rickshaw began to move, I came out of my hiding and began running after it. But the rickshaw was gaining speed, and not to lose it I clung to the iron guard attached to the back of the vehicle. The rickshawman was forced to stop and then discovered the extra load he was pulling. Father laughed at my trickery, picked me up, and let me ride on his lap all the way. That's how I started my first day in school. The students gathered around and teased me, I recall, for I was wearing the traditional child's jacket with rainbow sleeves. I didn't mind; I was only too happy to be there.

I attended this school for three years, and the most vivid memory I have is of the day when the teachers cried before all the students at the daily assembly. All of us sat on the floor as usual and waited for the teacher to stand before us and lead us in singing our school songs.

"I have a special announcement to make today," the teacher said . . . and then halted abruptly as though he could not continue. After some moments of struggle to regain his composure, the teacher said, "By order of the Governor-General, at every assembly we must sing the Japanese patriotic song . . . in Japanese!"

"No! No! No!" some students shouted. The teacher held up his hand and said, "Unless we obey and sing the Japanese song, we won't be permitted to continue our school." All the teachers sitting on the platform broke into tears and the students on the floor froze into silence.

Finally, the teacher began teaching us the hated Japanese song. I still remember the concluding line of the chorus: *"Doho subete hijisen man"*—"Our countrymen altogether now number seventy million." Japan was not content with adding thirty million Koreans to the forty million Japanese—we were forced to sing it everyday in school. I could never forget the tears my teacher shed as he taught us to repeat the chorus over and over again.

But my childhood was not always so sad. In fact, there were many happy days, especially in the springtime when all the snow melted away, the freezing wind stopped blowing, and the sun grew warmer. In the streets, the long rows of poplar trees sprouted new leaves, the hills put on new pale green covers, and all the animals and the birds pranced and fluttered restlessly. And that was when Papa and Umma would plan our springtime family picnic. Umma and Eun-Yim's mother, our caretaker's wife, would spend the whole day and night preparing the picnic feast while the children would gather around them and relive the outing we had had the year before.

The excitement of our picnic day began at dawn. Of course we would all get up early, put on our traveling clothes and straw sandals, and hurry through our breakfast. For once, we children were ready long before the elders gathered all the paraphernalia for the picnic. Finally, when Umma announced "All right, we are ready!" we dashed out and led the way past the familiar West Gate Road and headed for the mountain. We would soon leave the city streets behind and begin climbing the narrow, winding mountain path. When we reached higher ground, the whole scenery changed. We were surrounded by all kinds of wildflowers and a profusion of yellow, white, and pink azaleas. We came to a stream rushing noisily through a bed of pebbles and rocks. Everyone stopped, drank the clear water with cupped hands, and sat on the sun-warmed rocks to rest.

We resumed climbing and finally found the ideal spot for our picnic. It was a spacious clearing encircled by gnarled, old pine trees and wild peach trees in full bloom. Clusters of azaleas splashed bright pink blossoms against the odd-shaped dark boulders. Eun-Yim's father, our caretaker, who had carried my invalid sister all the way up the mountain, put her down on a straw mat. He then led us to a grove of weeping willows whose long slender branches touched the stream flowing below. He cut a willow branch, gently peeled off its skin without damaging it, and shaped one end like the reed of a flute. He made one for each of us but of different lengths to blow different sounds. When we blew our reeds all at the same time, they sounded almost like the *piri* of the royal musicians. Reeds ablowing, we scattered over the hillside to pick tender fern sprouts and dandelion shoots and dig up *do-ra-ji,* the ginseng-like white roots which grew among the rocks. Umma would eventually prepare these mountain plants into an irresistible springtime delicacy.

We never knew what our caretaker's name was. He and his family had lived with us for many years in the "Gate Watcher's House," a little house built next to the main gate. He had a pretty daughter, named Eun-Yim, a year or two older than I was. As was often customary, everyone was called according to his or her relation to the child. So the caretaker was always Eun-Yim's father; his wife, Eun-Yim's mother; and their son, Eun-Yim's brother. Eun-Yim's father was a ne'er-do-well pleasure-loving man who spent the days away from home and returned in the evening, usually very drunk. Embarrassed and ashamed, Eun-Yim's mother would try to keep him indoors, but he would stagger out and want to play with us children. I would imitate his stuttering and wobbling and run around him in circles trying to make him fall down.

Eun-Yim's brother was rather slow-witted, and everyone treated him with indifference. Eun-Yim's mother was my favorite. She was beautiful and lively, and she always laughed merrily at her own stories. She was Umma's indispensable helper: housecleaning, laundering, sewing, and cooking. But at the end of the day, when she put me to bed, I would have her all to myself. She would tell me the most fascinating stories and lull me to sleep. Occasionally, she would let her daughter, Eun-Yim, lie down with me. Oh, what pleasure! Under cover of the cotton-padded blanket, my hand would slowly reach out and touch her, and, ever so cautiously, explore her body while she did the same with mine. So it was under the quilt that I first discovered the intriguing secrets of a girl.

Our picnic was now in full swing. To me, there is nothing that smells as wonderful as Korean *bul-go-gee,* the thin slices of marinated beef broiling on a charcoal fire. Whenever *bul-go-gee* was cooking, the whole surrounding area came alive with an aroma which aroused everyone's appetite. We also had a special rice called *bee-bim-bap,* cooked white rice mixed with shredded cucumber, bean sprouts, mushrooms, and a dab of hot soybean sauce. Besides, there were *go-sa-ri* (fern shoots), *kong-na-mul* (soybean sprouts), *do-ra-ji* (springtime roots), and, of course, several kinds of *kim-chee* (pickled cabbage). What a feast! What a heavenly picnic!

When the lunch was over, we trekked up the hill following the stream until we reached the spot where the water was gushing out of the cracks in the rocky mountain. Eun-Yim's father caught the water in a large bottle and passed it around.

"Drink it, children! Drink! Drink!" Umma urged us, "It's *yak-mul*—medicine water!" I didn't care to drink too much of the "medicine water" even though I was assured it would make me strong and free of any sickness. Afterwards, we returned to our picnic ground, took our seats on straw mats, and listened to Papa's stories. They were usually about a brave tiger hunter, about a poor farmer who became rich through honesty and hard work, or about an evil man who lost all his fortune through his greed. Then at the request of the elders, the children sang all our favorite folk songs. I was always asked to sing a solo—my favorite, the students' marching song. And Papa would respond by leading us in singing his favorite hymn, "Onward Christian Soldiers." He would then offer a prayer of thanks, always remembering to ask for God's blessing for his people and his country. Trudging home tired but happy, I would tug at Umma's sleeve and ask, "Umma, when are we going to have another picnic?"

"Next spring." She would pat my head and laugh silently.

Another childhood diversion which I remember so well are my visits to Umma's parents' home. The old Korean custom dictated that when a girl married and moved to her husband's home, she should cut off all ties with her own family. Even her parents are relegated to second-class status, and her children call them not grandfather and grandmother but Wei-Ga-Jip Hal Abuji and Wei-Ga-Jip Hal Munni— "Other House" Grandfather and "Other House" Grandmother. Defying such edicts, Umma would take us to the home of her parents for visits, but always after dark. Dr. Lee, her father, was the Royal Physician and was forbidden to give any medical service outside the palace. So whenever one of us got sick, Umma took us to see the doctor after dark. He was a gentle and kind man, and Umma's mother was a tiny, pretty lady. I could see where Umma inherited her slight, delicate features.

My "Other House" grandparents were always glad to see me and would shower me with all sorts of presents, not to mention the carefully wrapped coins for my pouch. My pleasure would be dampened somewhat when I had to lie on the floor and submit to an examination by my "Other House" grandfather. Then, in fascination, I would watch him grinding an ink stone on his tiny table, pick up a brush in his delicate hand, and write a mysterious inscription on a piece of rice paper: the prescription for my ailment, without the customary seal of the doctor so that its source would not be revealed. That was the distasteful part of otherwise most delightful visits to my "Other House" grandparents, for when we returned home late at night, I would have to swallow the bitter brew of the herb medicine.

But the most exciting holiday of my childhood was the New Year's—not the January First on the calendar, but a different day of February each year, according to the ancient lunar calendar. Days before the *real* New Year, as we used to call it, Umma, Eun-Yim's mother, and neighborhood ladies would buzz around the kitchen preparing all the innumerable New Year delicacies: rice nectar, honey-soaked chestnut rice, cake-rice cooked and pounded in a wooden barrel and then kneaded and rolled into thin bars. The bars were stored until New Year's morning when they would be sliced into little strips and cooked in rich beef soup. It was said that unless a bowl of this *duk-guk*—"cake soup"—was eaten on New Year's Day, a Korean could not add another year to his life.

The days before New Year were just as exciting and festive. As the ladies busied themselves peeling, chopping, and cutting while others were rolling, pounding, and stuffing, we children sat in a circle and played "Yoot," a very exciting ancient Korean game. In the center of the floor, we spread a square rice paper on which a racecourse was drawn. Each player had four horses—buttons or pebbles of different colors—and the one who ran all four horses through the course first would be the winner. The course consisted of twenty spaces around the square as well as twenty spaces in diagonal. The player might choose any route, but each horse had to cover all twenty spaces to finish the race.

The number of spaces a horse might jump was determined by a toss of the "Yoot": four pieces of finely carved sticks, each of which had a flat side and a round side. The player threw the sticks up and let them fall on the floor. The horse moved according to the number of flat sides facing up, from one to a maximum of four. But should the sticks fall with all the flat sides down, the horse could move five spaces.

The race became complicated because the front-running horse could be captured and sent back to the starting point if another horse landed on its space. Four or five players yelling and screaming for the desired number to capture a horse could create quite a commotion! The excitement was made all the more intense by the fact that the losers had to pay the winner with the nuts and candies everyone had received from Umma for the daily ration.

Everything had to be settled before midnight of the last day of the old year, including all old debts. Failure to do so would not only besmirch the family name but also bring misfortune throughout the New Year. It was also very important for us children to stay awake for the arrival of the New Year. If any of us should fall asleep before midnight and let the New Year come while we slept, Umma would warn us that in the morning we would find our eyebrows turned as white as snow. This frightened me and though exhausted from the daylong excitement and my eyes heavy with sleep, I would struggle to stay awake.

"Pedro-ya, don't fall asleep!" Startled by Umma's voice, I would blink my eyes open and mumble, "No, Umma, I'm not sleeping. . . ." The burst of laughter from all the ladies would fully awaken me so that I could keep my vigil and be sure to find my eyebrows unwhitened on New Year's Day.

At last! The dawn of New Year's Day! As if by a miracle, Umma would present each of her eight children with a new suit of clothes. In these beautiful new outfits, our first duty was to offer the New Year greetings to our father and mother. Taking turns from the oldest to the youngest, we would make our traditional bows before them. As rewards, Papa would hand each of us a precious coin—the first one to go into my new embroidered silk pouch which I looped around my belt.

We then ate our New Year breakfast—the indispensable *duk-guk* without which we could not add another year to our age. It was now time for us older children to go and pay homage to all the elders. Eun-Yim's father would escort us on our daylong trip, first to Grandfather and "Other Room" Grandmother, then to our uncles and aunts whose homes were scattered around the city. At each stop, my two older sisters and I would enter the main room where the elders awaited the children's New Year visits. There we would perform the traditional bows.

For proper execution of this formal bow, the girl needed agility and balance. Very slowly, she had to bend her knees and lower herself to the floor without falling back. At the same time, her hands were kept at the side of her legs, which, of course, were hidden inside her full skirt, until the hands slowly reached down and touched the floor. She then tilted her head and cast her eyes downward. Still maintaining her balance, she then had to reverse her movement and arise without losing the rhythm. The entire bow was performed in one flowing graceful motion. There were times when I tried to imitate this girl's bow, but I always lost my balance and fell over, sending my sisters into fits of laughter.

By comparison, the boy's bow was quite easy. I knelt, extended my arms, and placed both hands together on the floor. I then bent over from my waist until my forehead touched the back of my hands. After a moment, I would straighten and rise. The ceremony was over. Now we would be treated to the New Year delicacies. Just as for grown-ups, a little table would be set before us, loaded with cakes, sweets, and fruits. But the best moment came when, as we were about to leave, we received the New Year coins prettily wrapped in red paper which I quickly dropped into my pouch. Walking around the city and repeating the ceremony at every stop, I lost all appetite for delicacies and my legs would begin to ache. But I didn't mind, for the pouch was getting fuller and heavier. Upon returning home, the first thing I did was to empty it and count the coins. There were so many, Umma had to take some away for safekeeping.

For me, the second day of the New Year was even busier than the first. I had to hurry through my breakfast and dash out to meet my neighborhood friends. Each one would tell his story of New Year's Day: how much food he ate, how many times he had to kneel and bow, and most important of all how many coins he had amassed at the end of the day. I was ready to spend some of my New Year fortune as quickly as possible, and I knew just where to spend it. Accompanied by a band of boys, I would rush to the kite shop. First, I would pick a sturdy wooden spindle with a long handle at one end. Then I would get several spools of extra-strong cotton thread, one package of glue powder, and, finally, the most beautiful kite I could find; it had red, yellow, and green bands and fierce-looking eyes painted in the upper corners. On the way home, we would pick up all the broken glass we could find on the road.

Returning home, we had many things to do. First, someone had to boil the package of glue in a pot while somebody else wound the thread onto my new spindle. Still others got busy dumping the pieces of glass we had found into a metal bowl and pounding them with a piece of stone until they became glass dust. While the thread was being held down in the pot of hot glue, it was wound onto another spindle. Then the thread was held down in the pot of glass dust and wound back onto my spindle. This was repeated once more to make certain the thread was tough and sharp as a knife. We were now ready to do battle with any kite that dared challenge us.

Our troupe climbed up to the battleground at the top of the hill where all the kite fliers gathered. "Hey, look at that funny-looking kite!" Some boys jeered at us, "Did you ever see such an ugly kite? Can it fight?" Pretending not to have heard them, I put the kite in the air for its maiden flight; it flew gracefully and rose with great dignity. I then put it through the test of fighting maneuvers. By manipulating the spindle, I could guide my kite to sweep across to the right, and then reverse itself to the left. By very fast spinning of the spindle, I could make the kite soar straight up until it could climb no more. That was the moment to pull the line suddenly and make the kite turn upside down. Rapid pulling of the line in this position would make the kite dive straight down until the line became slack and the kite turned upward again. With every successful maneuver, my friends jumped and clapped happily.

"Look out, Pedro-ya!" I heard someone yell and at the same instant saw a kite swooping down on mine. I had to maneuver quickly to let my kite dive and fly away from the attacker. I led my kite to soar high and fly over the attacker, but it too escaped. We repeated this cat-and-mouse game several times while the boys on both sides yelled and screamed. Finally I made a daring move. I lured the enemy kite into attacking me, and when it did, instead of retreating, I raised my kite straight up. When I gained the upper hand, I dived my kite and let my razor-sharp line pass over the enemy line. It was cut instantly and the enemy kite floated away helplessly. My friends' victory yells pierced the hillside.

At times, the kite battles resembled a small war as one neighborhood would challenge another for kite flying supremacy. At such an event, the grown-ups took charge of the flying. Their preparations were elaborate: hugh spindles, tough sharp threads, and specially designed kites. These kites, according to their colors and decorations, would be given nicknames such as "Blue Nose," "Red Skirt," and "Tiger Eyes." At the height of the battle, adults as well as children would be screaming.

"Watch out, Blue Nose!"

"Red Skirt, get away! Get away, Red Skirt!"

"Chase him, Tiger Eyes! Chase him!"

All through the day, with each victory of the heated battles, the yells and screams reverberated over the hills.

The New Year celebrations lasted fifteen days until the first full moon, but they seemed to pass all too quickly. Fortunately, there were other pleasurable days of my childhood which were more enduring such as the days of my visits to my grandparents. They lived in a big house at the foot of a hill surrounded by many hectares of field which were cultivated by farmhands who lived on the land. My grandmother was always called Am-Bang Grandmother—"Other Room" Grandmother. I didn't know why until one day Umma explained it to me. Our real grandmother, my father's mother, had died, and Grandfather married again. We were then taught to call this new grandmother, to distinguish her from the real one, "Other Room" Grandmother. I particularly remember my visits on hot summer days. Grandfather would call the farmhands and ask them to cook some fresh corn for his grandson. Soon they would bring a bundle of corn from the fields and build a fire under a huge cauldron filled with water; when it began to boil, all the corn would be thrown in. When they were done, the farmhands would give me one ear of corn after another until I couldn't eat one more kernel. I have never eaten corn as sweet and delicious as that from Grandfather's fields.

"Pedro-ya!" I heard Grandfather calling me one day.

"*Nyee!* Yes, sir!" I answered, and I hurried and sat down before him.

"Pedro-ya, you are now eight years old," he said in a serious tone.

"*Nyee,* Grandfather."

"About time you should learn about your ancestors."

"*Nyee,* Grandfather."

"Do you know who the founder of the Hyun family is?"

"No, Grandfather."

"His name is Hyun Dam-Yun, a great general in the era of King Myung Chong of the Koryu kingdom. To honor his great fame, we inscribe his name as founder of the Hyun family."

"Did he fight many battles, Grandfather?"

"He was not always a general. In fact he was a common farmer living in the village of Yong-Byun in the northern province of Pyong-An."

"Then how did he become a general?"

"It happened nearly eight hundred years ago. The king's throne was threatened by one of his governors and the king had to flee. Farmer Hyun Dam-Yun learned that the king was in hiding near his village and decided to help him. Together with his two sons, he formed a large army of farmers, fought the traitor and his followers, and finally defeated them soundly. In thankful recognition of his military talents, the king conferred upon Hyun Dam-Yun the title of general and appointed him his commander-in-chief. Hyun's two sons were also given high positions, and a great tract of land together with the rank of nobility was granted to the Hyun family. . . ."

"What happened to all the land, Grandfather, and why aren't we noblemen anymore?"

"Well, the Hyun family lost their title and all their land when the Koryu kingdom was overthrown five hundred years ago. And the Hyuns, still loyal to their king, refused to serve the new rulers under the Yi kingdom."

"Then what happened, Grandfather?"

"For five generations, the Hyuns lived quietly in the country as farmers." At this point, my mind began to drift, wondering how much more fun it would be to be listening to my great-grandmother's folktales instead.

"*Ee-nom-ah!* Hey, you!" I was startled by Grandfather's angry voice. "Why aren't you listening?" he admonished.

"Yes, I am. . . . I am listening, Grandfather. . . ." I answered weakly.

"Well, never mind," Grandfather sounded resigned. "That's enough for today. Go! Go and play, Pedro-ya. . . ." I was glad to sneak away and look for Great-Grandmother and her funny stories.

But from repeated sessions with Grandfather, and sometimes with Father, I learned of the rebuilding of the Hyun's family fortune. The new hero was the son of a humble farmer who carted firewood to Seoul for sale. He was befriended by a gentleman named Whang who happened to be in the diplomatic service of the government. Whang was impressed by this young country boy, with his family lineage, his knowledge of the Chinese classics, and his bright mind. In time, Whang proposed marriage with his daughter. Soon afterward, he took his son-in-law into the government diplomatic service. Thereafter, the Hyuns became known as the "Family of Diplomats." At the height of their career, Hyuns held important positions in foreign service such as that of attaché to the Korean ambassador to China and that of personal courier to the king.

My father's grandfather, the distinguished advisor to Prince Tai Won-Kun, had three wives. The first died without an heir; the second wife left four sons, the oldest being Hyun Chei-Sung, the famed diplomat. The third wife had one son, Chei-Chang, who became Papa's father. The Hyun's family history encompassed twenty-eight generations, and at the time of the March First uprising in 1919 it had covered the span of seven hundred eighty-nine years. In my generation, as the oldest of four sons I had the responsibility of carrying on all the family traditions. In my childhood I wasn't aware of such a grave responsibility and even less of any possible ill feeling among my younger brothers because of my position of honor in the family.

Perhaps I shouldn't have taken it for granted that I was my grandfather's favorite grandson and enjoyed to the full all the favors heaped upon me. Following time-honored custom, Grandfather would invite me to sit at his table and share his dinner. It meant not only the honor but also the privilege of tasting all the special foods prepared for him. And I would brag about it afterward to all my brothers and sisters. How jealous and resentful they all must have felt! Moreover, on cold winter nights when the chilly wind seeped through the paper-covered windows, I would be kept warm by being allowed to sleep between Grandfather and Am-Bang Grandmother.

To prepare for the night, a mattress would be spread out on the floor nearest to the kitchen, the warmest spot in the room; that was for Grandfather. Then another mattress would be spread next to it for Am-Bang Grandmother. I would crawl in between them where it was warm and secure. I had even greater rewards; when Am-Bang Grandmother lay down to sleep, I would turn to her and touch her breast. Oh, it felt so smooth and warm! Sometimes, she would let me hold onto her breast until I fell asleep. On one such winter night, I turned over in my sleep and accidentally touched Grandfather's penis. Startled even in my sleep, I quickly withdrew my hand. Then I was overwhelmed by curiosity. Now, consciously, I nudged my hand until I could touch it again. It felt good but not as good as Am-Bang Grandmother's breast. My curiosity satisfied, I would lose interest in the game and go back to sleep. Those winter nights when I nestled between my grandparents to find comfort and pleasure were among the unforgettable memories of my childhood.

4

GREAT-
GRANDMOTHER

To be sure, there were other incentives for my visits to Grandfather's. One of the important inducements was what I called the "Pennies Ritual" which took place at the end of my visit. When I was ready to leave, Am-Bang Grandmother would take my hand and press a few copper pennies in the palm. And as she closed my hand, she would say, "Listen, Pedro-ya. If you should get hungry before reaching home, stop and buy something to eat."

How well she knew me! At the halfway point, I would be seized with pangs of hunger for that was where I passed the row of street vendors. The whole street was filled with the smell of food, and it became irresistible when I reached the vendors roasting sweet potatoes and chestnuts. I gladly spent the copper pennies Am-Bang Grandmother had given. Oh, the roasted chestnuts and sweet potatoes! These were my favorite midway snacks during autumn and winter, but with the change of season the smell of the vendors' street also changed. In the spring and summer, it would be filled with the delicate scent of fruits: cherries, apricots, peaches and pears, and, later in the season, all kinds of melons. Now all the copper pennies I had received from Am-Bang Grandmother would be handed over to the vendors of cherries and apricots.

There were times, though not often, when the Pennies Ritual ran into a snag. Am-Bang Grandmother would forget it and I then faced the grim prospect of walking home without the usual stop at the vendors' row. To rectify the situation, I had to resort to melodrama. Outside the main gate, I would throw myself against the wall and break into a heartrending sob. I knew if Am-Bang Grandmother could not hear the tragic cry, some neighbor was sure to notice and report it. To make sure, I kept up my sobbing until Am-Bang Grandmother appeared in distress. To make up for her forgetfulness, she would press into my hand many more pennies than usual. Recovering quickly from the near tragedy, and forgiving Am-Bang Grandmother for her mistake, I would start walking my way home. Already my mind was at the vendors' row smelling and tasting all the delicious food I would have. My only problem was not being able to decide what to spend the money for: on the juicy autumn pears or the delectable persimmons.

These snacks at the vendors' which I relished so much were, of course, only fleeting pleasures. I found more enduring delight in listening to Great-Grandmother's folktales. She lived in a room of her own at Grandfather's. When I entered, I would usually find her sitting on a warm cotton mattress reading a book, invariably a popular novel. She would put her book down and motion for me to come closer. Happily I would stretch out on the floor, my hands cupped under my chin, ready to listen to another of her stories. She had a round, open face, warm and kind, and her eyes twinkled with whimsy and quiet laughter. Her storytelling in an even, warm voice always excited me in anticipation of adventure and mystery.

And when she finished the story, always concluding with a lesson in bravery, humor, or wisdom, I would immediately ask her, "Oh, Great-Grandmother, another story. Just one more story! Please, one more!" She would draw me closer so that I could rest my head on her lap and begin another story which like all the others sounded like it had happened only the day before. Of course I could never be satisfied, and when she finished, I would ask for still another one. I was sure her supply was inexhaustible and felt certain that when she died she still had many untold stories. The ones she did tell me made deep impressions, and I cherish them and the image of my great-grandmother as rare treasures of my childhood.

Among all the wonderful stories, one of my favorites was the story of "The Gentleman Farmer and the Tiger." Whenever I remembered it, I could see my great-grandmother's face reflecting the changes of mood and hear her deep voice which sounded so ominous and mysterious. This was the story:

Once upon a time, long, long ago, there lived a Gentleman Farmer in a little village. His large and prosperous farm was in the foothills of a soaring mountain, and on the mountain lived many ferocious tigers. Those beautiful but dangerous tigers always stayed in an inaccessible part of the mountain, but in the winter when they were driven by hunger, they would leave their mountain lairs and venture down to the village in search of food. Fortunately, the raids of the wild tigers were infrequent, and having well secured his home and the stables, the Gentleman Farmer hardly ever worried about the tigers.

Because he was a gentleman farmer, he never touched the field work; it was all done for him by his farmhands. He occupied himself instead with refining his mind by studying the Chinese classics and composing and reciting poetry. He also believed in keeping his body as healthy as his mind. For this purpose, he drank the bitterest brew of the rarest herbs and conducted the most rigorous exercises. In the winter hunting season, if he happened to kill a deer with his bow and arrow, he would chop off its horns on the spot and drink the hot gushing blood. Indeed, all these rituals had made him so strong that when there was a house on fire, the Gentleman Farmer would toss the men up onto the roof to put out the fire.

Well, one cold winter night, he was awakened by a strange noise. He had never heard anything like it before, and he listened and listened, trying to decide what it might be. It wasn't only the strange sound— *Clump! Clump! Clump!*—but its rhythmic regularity that fascinated him. *Clump! Clump! Clump!* Then silence. *Clump! Clump! Clump!* Then again silence. And on and on. . . . Now the Gentleman Farmer was fully awake and decided to solve the mystery. He got up and dressed and then stepped outside.

At this point, I would be so carried away I would clutch at Great-Grandmother's legs and implore, "Oh, what happened? What happened? Please, Great-Grandmother, hurry. Hurry and tell me what happened."

"What are you afraid of, Pedro-ya?" Great-Grandmother would tease me in her calm voice. "I haven't even started telling you about the real excitement yet."

"But please hurry, Great-Grandmother, hurry."

"If you would keep quiet and listen," she would still tease me, "I'll tell you what happened." And the story continued. . . .

The Gentleman Farmer finally traced the strange noise to the barn. He approached it stealthily and was startled by the loud *Clump! Clump! Clump! Clump!* Fortunately the bright moonlight helped him to see that it was his prize cow who was making all the noise by jumping up and down, up and down. But what was making her so nervous and frightened? To his amazement, he saw that a giant snake on the floor was whipping the cow's legs and making her jump up and down, up and down. But then, taking a closer look, he discovered that it wasn't a snake; it was a fat furry thing with black rings around it. The Gentleman Farmer knew that it could only be a tiger's tail!

A very hungry tiger had ventured down to the village in search of food only to find all the livestock locked up in the barn. Finding a knothole in the wooden wall, the tiger slid its tail through it and began whipping the cow's legs, hoping to frighten the cow and induce her to come out of the barn. So when the tiger swished its tail back and forth, back and forth, the frightened cow jumped up and down, up and down: *Clump! Clump! Clump! Clump!* A moment of silence and then the swish of the tiger tail, and again *Clump! Clump! Clump! Clump!*

The Gentleman Farmer quietly led the cow out of the barn. He then tiptoed back into the barn and quietly sat down on the floor, bracing his feet against the wall on either side of the knothole. In one lightning move, he snatched the tiger's tail, wound it around his forearm, and reared back with all of his strength as he let out a ground-shaking grunt, *"Yeeeh-Huuump!"*

Stunned by the predicament, the tiger tried to pull its tail out of the hole with a mighty roar, *"Grrraaahhh!"*

The Gentleman Farmer was jerked against the wall but held on to the tiger's tail. This was the moment of supreme challenge to his strength and courage. With a deep breath, he heaved and pulled the tiger's tail back: *"Yeeeh-Huuump!"*

The tiger responded with equal desperation: *"Grrraaahhh!"*

Neither the Gentleman Farmer nor the tiger would give up the struggle, and all through the night it went on:

"Yeeeh-Huuump!"

"Grrraaahhh!"

GREAT-GRANDMOTHER

"Yeeeh-Huuump!"
"Grrraaahhh!"
Back and forth, back and forth, and back and forth.

Then came the dawn, and as the day was breaking, the farmhands were awakened by the strange muffled rumbles—*"Yeeeh-Huuump!"* *"Grrraaahhh!"*—over and over again. They gathered in the courtyard and decided to find out where the noise was coming from. They opened the gate and went outside, and near the stable wall they beheld an unbelievable sight. An enormous tiger was sitting with its rear against the wall, and when a feeble cry came from inside the barn—*"Yeeeh-Huuump!"*—the tiger would move its rear closer to the wall. Then the tiger would roar weakly—*"Grrraaahhh!"*—at the same time, moving its rear forward. It kept repeating this most untiger-like behavior over and over. But strangest of all, the farmhands noticed that the tiger had no tail.

The farmhands scurried inside and rushed to the barn. There they found their master, the Gentleman Farmer, sitting on the floor with his legs propped up against the wall; he seemed as exhausted as the tiger outside. But when he heard the tiger's weak cry—*"Grrraaahhh!"*—he bent forward against the wall. Then he would lean back and grunt weakly, *"Yeeeh-Huuump!"* The movements and the barely audible cries of the tiger and the Gentleman Farmer continued on at regular intervals. The farmhands then became completely mystified by the sight of a loose tiger's tail dangling around the Gentleman Farmer's forearm.

I was puzzled and asked Great-Grandmother, "How did the tail come off the tiger?"

"Yei-ya—Yey, you," she answered calmly. "If you had a tail, Pedro-ya, and had it rubbed against a knothole all night, it would have come off, too." I exploded with laughter and rolled on the floor, clapping and kicking. Poor tiger, he didn't know his tail had come off, and poor Gentleman Farmer, he kept straining himself and grunting with a loose tiger's tail around his arm.

But when I had recovered from my laughing spasm, I would pull Great-Grandmother's legs and beg, as usual, "Great-Grandmother, one more story, please. Just one more story!" Sometimes the stories just seemed to be spinning out of her head, being made up as they went along. No matter, they never failed to be intriguing, exciting, and funny. Another story which made an everlasting impression on me was called the "Three Suffering Men."

Once upon a time, there lived in a farming village Three Suffering Men. By virtue of, or rather by the misfortune of, their sufferings, their fame spread through all the villages far and near. They would not have become so renowned had their sufferings come from some ordinary ailment such as a stomachache or from indigestion, a sore throat, a cold, or a pain in the foot from a cut. No, for the Three Suffering Men, the kinds of pain as well as their causes were most extraordinary.

For Farmer Lee, the suffering was in his head—not inside but all over the top of his head. Some strange affliction, which no doctor could diagnose, caused a severe and constant itch in his scalp. To find relief from this maddening itch, Farmer Lee spent all of his waking moments scratching his head; scratching, scratching, and scratching, sometimes with both of his hands. Working in the field, he would have to drop the hoe and scratch his head every few moments. And when a neighbor passing by greeted him, "Good morning, Farmer Lee, how are you?", he would politely bow scratching his head. "Good," scratch, scratch, "morning," scratch, scratch. "I'm just," scratch, scratch, "fine," scratch, scratch. "Thank," scratch, scratch, "you," scratch, scratch.

For Farmer Kim, his suffering was as excruciating but in an entirely different part of his body; it was not on top of his head but in his nostrils. Some strange malady which no doctor could cure caused his nose to run. In fact, the flow was so constant that even a towel proved inadequate. Instead, the upper parts of his sleeves were well padded so that he could wipe away the unpleasant drippings. When working in the field he would have to drop the hoe every so often and wipe his nose with both arms. And when a neighbor passing by greeted him, "Good morning, Farmer Kim. How are you?", he would bow politely and quickly wipe his nose. He would then respond, "Good," wipe, wipe, "morning," wipe, wipe. "I'm just," wipe, wipe, "fine," wipe, wipe. "Thank," wipe, wipe, "you," wipe, wipe.

It was yet another mystery for Farmer Cho; his head didn't itch, his nose didn't run, but, oh, his eyes! They were a honeypot for all the flies; wherever Farmer Cho went, the flies followed and swarmed around his eyes. In vain, the doctors tried different medicines to repel the insects. Then, at the advice of a Buddhist monk, Farmer Cho made a pilgrimage to a temple where he prayed and burned sticks of incense, but the flies swarmed over his eyes more than ever. There was nothing left for Farmer Cho to do but keep waving his hands in front of his eyes to chase the flies away: wave, wave, wave. The nuisance of the flies did not abate when Farmer Cho was working in the field; he had to put down the hoe and wave his hands to chase away the flies. And when a neighbor passing by hailed him, "Good morning, Farmer Cho! How are you?" Farmer Cho would bow politely while waving his hands in front of his face. Then he would respond, "Good," wave, wave, "morning," wave, wave. "I'm just," wave, wave, "fine," wave, wave. "Thank," wave, wave, "you," wave, wave.

Following the hot summer days, when the harvest was done, it was time for the Autumn Festival when all the farmers could put away their hoes as well as their worries and assemble for a day of celebration. And, as usual, the elders of the village met to discuss and plan the events for the festival. While drinking hot rice wine and smoking long bamboo pipes, they reviewed all the wonderful festivals they had held in the village in the past. But at the same time, they agreed that it was of little interest merely to repeat the same events year after year: singing, dancing, and storytelling. For once, they wished they could have an unusual and exciting event at the festival.

A young man among the elders, who was there to take the place of his deceased father, coughed shyly to draw the elders' attention. The leading elder pointed with his bamboo pipe allowing the young man to speak. The young man bowed and presented his idea for the feature event for the festival. The elders were impressed, and despite their reluctance to adopt the suggestion of such a young man, they could not reject such an intriguing idea. Thus the major event of the festival was announced: "The Tournament of the Three Suffering Men." They had no idea the announcement would stir up such furor and excitement not only in their own village but among all the surrounding villages. The farmers and their families could hardly wait for the day of the Autumn Festival.

Finally, the day of the festival arrived. From early in the morning, the people from all the villages began gathering. Carrying bundles of food and drink, men, women, and children settled on the hillside which surrounded the village mall. When the village gong struck the hour of noon, the group of elders marched into the mall, elegant and dignified in their holiday finery. The senior elder stepped forward and waved his fan signaling for silence.

"My most respected fellow farmers. . . ." The elder then paused for the children to quiet down. "Today, we are here to witness a most extraordinary tournament." A torrent of applause filled the air. "This is a Grand Tournament," the elder continued, "a challenge of man's willpower, patience, and endurance. The contestants in this historic contest are our own fellow farmers: Farmer Lee, Farmer Kim, and Farmer Cho, the famous Three Suffering Men, and here they are!" An outburst of applause, even more deafening, greeted the Three Suffering Men as they marched in, scratching, scratching; wiping, wiping; waving, waving. The crowd stood up, some applauding and some grimacing in pity.

"These Three Suffering Men," the elder shouted over the rumblings of the crowd, "besides their sufferings, also share another thing in common . . . their consummate love for pumpkin cake." The people clapped their hands in approval. "So," the elder continued, "as the just reward for the winner, we have baked a giant pumpkin cake." At the wave of his fan, four men appeared carrying a wooden platform which held an enormous claypot from which the sweet aroma of steaming pumpkin cake floated out. They set the platform down in the center of the mall as the people yelled and cheered. Then the Three Suffering Men were led to sit on a straw mat facing each other around the cake.

Now the elder proclaimed the final instructions. "At the signal of my fan," he said solemnly, "the Three Suffering Men must remain motionless. Farmer Lee must not scratch his itchy head; Farmer Kim must not wipe his running nose; and Farmer Cho must not wave his hands to chase the flies. The one who succumbs will be eliminated and the one who remains motionless the longest will be declared the winner and this beautiful pumpkin cake will be his prize." The people stirred and fidgeted and the Three Suffering Men, for their final relief, frantically scratched and scratched, wiped and wiped, and waved and waved. But when the elder swung his fan and bellowed "Now!" the Three Suffering Men froze instantly. So did all the people on the hillside watching them.

A minute passed, five minutes, and then ten minutes went by. Yet the Three Suffering Men remained absolutely motionless. The crowd watched the man with the itchy head: obviously suffering an excruciating itch, but no scratching. They turned to the man with the running nose: disgustingly wet, but no wiping. And the man with the suppurating eyes: a great swarm of flies, but no waving. Another ten minutes passed, yet there was not a stir among the Three Suffering Men; no scratching, no wiping, no waving. The people watching them began to grow restless. Now some of them began to scratch their own heads, some wiped their noses, and others began waving their hands in front of their faces. As more time passed, the distress of the people, more than the Three Suffering Men, was mounting. Another ten minutes. Frantically now, the people were scratching, scratching their heads; wiping, wiping their noses; and waving, waving their hands. Even the children joined the frenzy. But not the Three Suffering Men; they remained calm and undisturbed.

The agonizing stillness was broken by a lone voice. It was Farmer Lee, the one with the itchy head. "It seems rather foolish," he said, "to be sitting here in silence while waiting for the outcome of this Grand Tournament." He raised his voice to a higher pitch and continued, "So, to help pass the time, let me tell you a story." The crowd heaved a sigh of relief and listened.

"As you all know," Farmer Lee began, "to come to this mall, I had to pass through the great pine forest which I have done many times." He paused and the people grew rapt. "But this morning," Farmer Lee's voice now dropped to a low pitch, "as I was walking through the same forest, I saw a strange animal . . . a strange deer. Instead of just two horns on each side of its head, this deer had a horn here," he pounded his head with his fingertips, "and a horn there," pounding his head again. "Another horn here and another horn there," he pounded his head some more. "As a matter of fact, it had horns all over his head," he finished the story with a flourish of pounding all over his head. Farmer Lee's face shone with an expression of complete relief.

"Ah, what a pity! What a pity!" It was the voice of Farmer Kim, the one with the running nose. All the people turned to him to listen.

"What a pity I wasn't there with you, Farmer Lee." Farmer Kim sounded painfully regretful. "As you all know," he continued, "I am an expert archer. Oh, what a pity I wasn't there with Farmer Lee with my bow and arrow. All I would have needed was just one clean shot. Like this. . . ." He lifted an imaginary bow in his left hand and an arrow in his right. Then slowly he pulled the bowstring, his sleeve neatly brushing across his wet nose. "Yes, I do believe I could have brought the strange creature down with just one clean shot . . . like this." With another neat brushing of his nose, Farmer Kim's face beamed with relief.

The sound of a loud cough turned the people's attention to Farmer Cho, who was doubling over with an apparent spasm of laughter. Regaining his control with an effort, he waved his hands across his face, saying, "I don't want to hear any more of this nonsense. He kept waving his hands, at the same time begging, "Please, please, no more, no more of this nonsense!" Wave, wave, wave. "I really don't want to hear any more nonsense." Everyone on the hillside understood the story perfectly. With a massive sigh of relief, the people began mimicking the Three Suffering Men. They pounded their heads screaming, "Yes, yes, yes! The strange deer had a horn here, a horn there, and horns everywhere all over his head! Yes, yes, yes, one clean shot with my bow and arrow! Just one clean . . . very clean shot!" The screams were deafening. "No more!" Wave, wave. "No more! No more of this nonsense!" Wave, wave, wave. . . .

The senior elder, a very wise man, sauntered to the center of the mall and waved his fan for silence. "My most respected farmers and neighbors," he droned each word slowly, "I declare this Grand Tournament to be at an end. And I further declare the three noble contestants to be all equal: equal in suffering, equal in endurance, and equal in wit." The people roared and applauded in approval. Once again, the elder waved his fan and the crowd fell silent.

"And in keeping with the spirit of this most unique contest," the elder took a deep breath, "I award this beautiful pumpkin cake in equal shares to the Three Suffering Men!" Humbly the three men stood and bowed in all directions, still scratching, scratching; wiping, wiping; and waving, waving. Then they cut the cake and passed it to everyone in the crowd, who, along with them, had suffered so much in the ordeal.

GREAT-GRANDMOTHER

Such were the wonderful stories my great-grandmother would tell me. I was eight years old when she died at the age of ninety-two. As the oldest son, I had the duty to formally represent my generation at the funeral. The traditional mourner's costume was made for me to wear: pantaloons, a shirt, and a tunic, all made of roughly woven and unbleached yellowish cotton. On the morning of the funeral, I stood in line with the elders to pay our last respects to Great-Grandmother. Everyone in line represented a generation and his family. When my turn came, I went into the room where she lay in state. For the first time in my life I found myself alone in a room with a dead person. But I was not afraid. I leaned and looked over the screen which shielded her. She way lying on the same cotton mattress on which she used to sit and tell me so many funny stories. Now her face was calm and deep in sleep with a little smile as though having an amusing dream. I stepped back, kneeled, and touched my head on the floor three times. How I would miss her, my beloved Great-Grandmother.

Another part of my duty was to accompany the bier on the walk to the cemetery. The Japanese rulers forbade burials in the ancestral burial grounds, and much to our family's humiliation, we were forced to bury our great-grandmother in the public cemetery. Nonetheless, she was given a rich and proud burial ceremony. The bier was carried by ten men dressed in mourner's costume with the white band around their heads. Behind the bier walked a long line of mourners from every Hyun family. The ladies, however, followed on rickshaws. The procession was accompanied by sad, rhythmic cries of the professional wailers. The funeral party halted at the halfway point. There was a large tent into which the ladies retired to escape the hot sun and rest. Refreshments and snacks were served to everyone.

When we finally arrived at the chosen site for the grave, the elders who had gathered by the graveside expounded on the wisdom of its selection. I couldn't understand all the complicated divination, but I could see them pointing in different directions and saying, "See, the sun rises over there, and from here there is a fine view of the Han River. In the summer, the rain could not flood this high ground, and in the winter, the high hill over there will protect the grave from severe winds." How wonderful, I thought, and felt grateful to the wise elders for choosing such a good grave for my beloved Great-Grandmother.

The coffin was lowered into the ground to lie in the exact designated position. The grave was filled, and over it a huge circular mound was built. To my surprise, the ladies carried a handsome lacquer table and set it before the grave, and other ladies brought plates and bowls and set a sumptuous meal on the table: a bowl of soup and rice, broiled fish and meat, and, of course, a colorful bowl of *kim-chee*. The ladies finished the setting by laying a pair of silver chopsticks and a silver spoon at the head of the table.

Something alarmed me, however. I went to Umma and pointed at the table. "Look, Umma, they put the soup on the left side of the rice. You told me that the soup must always be placed on the right side of the rice." She patted me gently and whispered, "Ah, but Great-Grandmother is now lying in the ground, looking up. Your left is her right."

5

LIFE WITHOUT FATHER

AFTER THE MEMORABLE EVENING at the South Gate railway station when our father took his leave, my life changed overnight. I graduated from the public elementary school and entered Bai Jai Hak Dang, the "Talent Blossoming Study Hall." To attend this great school and to wear the Bai Jai uniform had been one of my earliest childhood dreams. All my heroes in their splendid uniforms were there. The mighty athletes who played soccer and baseball, their proud walk when they entered Papa's church on Sundays; they were all from Bai Jai. But when I finally enrolled and became a Bai Jai student, it was not what I had dreamed. With Father gone, Umma did not have the money to buy my uniform, so I still wore the pantaloons and the long traditional tunic with only the Bai Jai school cap to show my new status. And I was too young and too small to play soccer or baseball.

Moreover, I had another special problem. Every now and then, on the way to and from school, I would be accosted by a stranger who would take me aside and with an unusual friendliness engage me in conversation. In the beginning, he would ask only some innocuous questions such as how I liked my new school and how was everyone in the family. When I reported these happenings to Umma, she said, "It's the Japanese police spy."

"What did they want of me?" I pondered.

"They are trying to find out about Papa . . . where he is and what he is doing."

"But, I don't know," I said.

"Just the same," Umma sounded ominous, "they will keep after you and try to make you a spy for them." Then she cautioned me, "Do not be hostile to them, but do not be too friendly either." It was then that I began to live a secretive life, a life of subterfuge and plotting. The Japanese police never gave up, however. The stranger now confronted me more frequently and became bolder.

"Have you heard from your father? Did you receive any letter from him? Who are his close friends? Where does your mother get the money for family food?" The queries became more and more personal and persistent.

One evening, Umma woke me from my sleep and begged me to get up. All the children were sound asleep. Umma took me to the corner at the end of the room and whispered.

"Listen, Pedro-ya. You cannot go to school anymore."

"Why, Umma?" I was alarmed.

"Because the police will keep after you and they will do something terrible to make you talk."

"But couldn't they do that even if I wasn't going to school?"

"We must convince them that we have no money . . . that nobody is helping us. That is why I have moved the family into this one-room house."

"All right, Umma." I tried to speak like a grown-up. "I'll go to work. I'll earn some money."

Umma looked at me with tears in her eyes. "Very good, Pedro-ya. Now you are the man of the family." With an effort I held back the tears that were welling inside of me at the thought of having to leave the Bai Jai Hak Dang.

The first moneymaking venture was a fulfillment of another one of my childhood dreams: to be a street vendor on the streets of the South Gate railway station. I found a partner, a boy older and bigger than I. Clutching a silver dollar with which Umma had entrusted me, we went to the big city market near the South Gate. I paid the whole dollar for a box of peaches. We couldn't afford the best, but the box we bought contained more peaches, and to me they looked big enough and luscious. My partner and I carried the box to the South Gate Road and found a shady spot under a tree. We spread a straw mat on the ground and laid our peaches on it in neat little piles. What a thrilling moment! At last I was a street vendor on the South Gate Road!

"Peaches! Peaches! Delicious peaches! Five cents! Only five cents!" We took turns hawking with enthusiasm and gusto. I was already counting the profit: five cents a peach, one hundred peaches, five dollars! Oh, I felt so proud and excited.

"Peaches! Delicious peaches! Five cents! Only five cents!"

The sun rose high and the day was approaching noon, yet we had not sold a single peach! Soon, both of us got hungry so we ate a few ourselves. I noticed the color of the peaches turning slightly. I became worried. Even if we now sold all the peaches, we could not earn five dollars. Dispelling the awful thought, we resumed hawking with renewed determination.

"Peaches! Delicious peaches! Five cents! Only five cents!" Still no buyers! What's wrong? I sent my partner down the street on a spying mission. He ran back and reported breathlessly, "Yes, they are selling peaches . . . but theirs are a lot bigger than ours . . . and cheaper!"

"Did you notice anyone buying them?"

"Ya! People were buying them!"

We changed our policy. We put three peaches in each pile and we changed our tune.

"Three peaches! Three delicious peaches for five cents! Only five cents for three peaches!" Some people actually stopped to look, but they walked on.

Now it became a very serious business. The hot afternoon sun was beating down, wilting my peaches, some of them showing sad, brown spots. We changed our policy again, now it was four peaches in each pile, and our tune: "Four peaches for five cents! Four peaches for only five cents!" I was beginning to feel a slight panic. I prayed, "Oh, please! Please, somebody buy my peaches!" No, praying did not help either. I decided to put two more peaches in each pile; we had to get rid of them somehow . . . even at a great loss. "Six peaches for five cents!" A terrible anger rose inside of me. Why wouldn't they buy my peaches? Why? "Six peaches for five cents! Six peaches for five cents!"

Our cry was losing its luster. The sun was setting, and people were scurrying home. They wouldn't even give a look at the peaches now. We didn't know what to do. It was already getting dark. We salvaged a few still edible peaches, and dumped the rest and the box into a ditch. When I arrived home, I handed over the few wilted peaches and shamefully reported, "Umma, the business was no good. . . . Don't know why they wouldn't buy my peaches. . . . I lost the whole dollar, Umma."

"Pedro-ya," Umma said in her comforting voice, "you know, a vendor's business is not easy. The vendors at the South Gate Road have been doing it many, many years. They know how to do it."

No more business. But I still had to earn some money. I'd heard of people working in a famous jewelry shop and I found the place. It was the old King's Arts Workshop where the master artisans produced all kinds of beautiful things: lacquer work, ceramics, pottery, and fine jewelry. It used to be known as the Royal Art Works, but of course it was now owned by the Japanese. What luck! I got hired as a jeweler's apprentice. My job was to assist the master jewelers with every kind of help they needed: checking out the precious metals, silver and gold, in the morning, firing the crucible and melting the amount of silver or gold the master wanted, and threading it through the metal gauge according to desired sizes. Sometimes, I held the hot metal with a vise for the master to pound in rhythmic beats. In time, I learned to turn and move the metal back and forth in the same rhythm as the master's hammer. After a few months, the master handed me a strand of gold and let me shape it into a ring. It turned out as a plain gold band, but I thought it was very beautiful. One of the masters was a Japanese who sang to himself all day as he worked. From him I learned my first Japanese song, which I can still sing to this day.

The most pleasant daily happening at work was the lunch break. I carried to work a large brass bowl wrapped in linen. The bowl would be filled with the delicious food Umma had prepared: rice, *kim-chee,* bean sprouts or cucumber salad, and, sometimes, surprises of bits of meat and fish. When the lunch bell rang, all the workers would go out of doors and sit wherever they could to eat their lunch. Once a week, however, Umma would let me have my lunch at the factory dining hall. For twenty-five cents, I had a bowl of fancy mixed rice with *kim-chee,* or a bowl of noodles in broth with *kim-chee.* But more often than not, I would order the complete lunch. The waiter would set a little lacquer table and spread a feast: a steaming bowl of rice, a bowl of turnip soup, a dish of broiled beef, a dish of fried fish patties, a plate of radish salad, and, of course, *kim-chee*. It was almost like my birthday meal. The grown-ups would look at me and laugh, "Look, look at the boy! He earns fifty cents a day and spends seventy-five cents for his lunch!" But I wouldn't let them bother me. I didn't care if I was too extravagant—Umma had given me her permission. Besides, the meal was so delicious and satisfying, and the Japanese police stopped bothering me and Umma was pleased.

Nevertheless, Umma never stopped being suspicious of the police following her wherever she went. She was particularly nervous when she and I would take a long night walk, usually once a week. Before we started, she would go to the gate and scan the neighborhood for any suspicious characters. When she was sure it was clear, she would signal me to join her. We would walk off in haste as though on an emergency errand. First, we would go straight to our uncle's house where we would be received with surprise. What were we doing out so late at night? After a sufficient lapse of time, we would emerge and resume our walk. Only then would Umma confide to me the address of the house we were headed for. But we would walk almost in the opposite direction. When we turned the corner, we would stop and wait to see if anyone was following. By a long and devious route, we would finally arrive at the house and knock on the door. We would then be led into a room where an elderly man would receive us and begin to speak to Umma.

I heard him tell Umma very politely that he did not have any money for her. Umma was even more polite when she informed him that, indeed, he had better have some money, because her children were starving. The polite conversation then changed into an argument. "You, a great leader of the revolution, listen to me." Umma would raise her voice in anger, "I know that money was left here for my family. Now give it to me." The man was speechless, and weakly tried to persuade Umma to wait awhile. "Wait? Wait for what? Wait until all my children die of starvation?" The man tried again, "Just a few more days . . . and I'll have the money for you. . . ." Then Umma really tore into him, "Listen, you miserable leader, I am not here begging, I am here to get the money that was entrusted to you to feed my family. My husband is giving his life for the revolution. Now you just give me the money." I felt sorry for the helpless man who got up and left the room. In amazement I looked at Umma, "Do you think he has any money?" "Of course." Umma was positive. "Just wait and see." Momentarily, the man returned and handed some money to Umma. She counted it carefully and said to the man, "This will do for a week. Thank you. I'll be back next week."

Near midnight, we would walk back home through narrow alleys and deserted dark streets. I was so overcome with Umma's fearlessness that I asked, "Umma, did you really know he had the money?" She replied, "Of course, I did. Listen, Pedro-ya, they collected an enormous amount of money for the independence movement. They divided and entrusted each sum to different leaders whose duty was to guard it and use the money to provide for the family of men like Papa who would never be able to come home." I was awed by the magnitude of this confidential information. Suddenly I realized that now I was part of the secret movement fighting for Korean independence. For nearly a year, at regular intervals, Umma and I journeyed on our midnight walks. And each time, Umma waged her fearless battle for the money that was meant to provide for us children.

I didn't know then that, more than once, Umma had been arrested by the police and subjected to intensive grilling. "Well, I just bared my fangs," she would tell me gleefully about her experience with the police. "You'd better let me go," she would challenge the police, "or you'd better go and feed my eight children." But life without Papa became more and more difficult: living in one room with eight growing children, the daily struggle to obtain food, the anxiety over Papa, and Umma's loneliness which grew each day and weighed on all of us. So, she made up her mind to leave Korea and to join Papa in China. But how? Even if we had the money to travel, the Japanese police would never give us the necessary permit to leave the country. As usual, Umma approached the problem directly—first things first. With all her ferocity, she was able to persuade the treasurer to give her six months' living expenses in one lump sum. Next, the police passport.

She knew an American missionary who was assigned to the Japanese church. It was rumored among the Koreans that he was a spy for the Japanese. Umma herself was certain that this missionary had an intimate contact with high Japanese officials. She and I searched and found his home and we went to visit him one evening. The missionary recognized Umma and invited us in. We sat stiffly on the American chairs. The room was filled with luxurious American furniture. Umma told the missionary the purpose of our visit. He did not know Korean but spoke fluent Japanese and I became the interpreter. Umma came straight to the point: My father had been gone for a year and she had managed to feed the children by begging at friends and relatives. But she couldn't do that any longer. She must take the family and go to Shanghai and find the children's father.

"You must help us," she declared.

"How can I help you?"

"By obtaining the necessary passport for us."

There was a long pause and then the missionary asked, "But how can I get the passport? It would be very difficult."

"Not for you. Besides, the Koreans will respect you if you help us." The missionary flinched at Umma's ploy.

"I'll see what I can do."

"Yes, please get the passport right away . . . hmmm . . . next week. I'll come back a week from tonight." Before the missionary could protest, Umma stood up and gave him a big smile, thanked him profusely, and rushed out of the house.

Returning home in the dark, I asked Umma, "Do you think he can get the passport?" "He will," she assured me, "and don't worry, Pedro-ya." When we returned the following week, it was the missionary who greeted us with a broad smile. He went to his desk and returned with a little booklet. He slapped his palm with it and then handed it to Umma. She accepted it gracefully and, hiding her surprise, she said, "Thank you so very much. I knew you were the only man in all Seoul who could get this for us."

6

THE JAPANESE

MY EARLIEST ENCOUNTERS with the Japanese were always at a distance, watching them furtively. I was taught by the elders, especially by Umma, not to trust the Japanese, not even the young. They were tricky and treacherous, I was told, and I should never come in close contact with them. On my way to and from school, however, I had to pass the Japanese school. The best I could do in this daily encounter was to walk on the opposite side of the Japanese, and when they occupied both sides, to choose the side with the least number of them. But no matter where I walked, whenever they passed me I would stiffen myself and try to ignore their jeers and laughter.

In spite of such hateful moments, I would carefully observe them. They were all in uniforms, the girls with short black skirts and white blouses in imitation of the Western style. Their hair, too, was uniformly cut: in the back, a straight line across their necks, and in the front, halfway down along their cheeks and bangs over their foreheads. Thus they resembled the Japanese dolls displayed in their shop windows. Imitating Western style, the boys wore black trousers and well-fitting tunics with brass buttons in the front. What impressed me was their shiny, black leather shoes, and I was also somewhat envious of the leather bags with straps which they carried across their shoulders. What a smart and luxurious way to carry books, pencils, and their *bendo,* the lunch box.

In contrast, I was dressed in Korean pantaloons with the bottoms tied around the ankles; over the short white blouse, I wore a long flowing tunic held together by a bow. Perched on my head was the black cap with the insignia of my school: *"OK"*—that is, JADE. I felt quite well dressed, as did all the other proud Korean students. But why did the Japanese always jeer and laugh at me? Because of my flimsy Korean sandals? Or was it the cloth bundle in which I carried my books and lunch?

At times, when there were no Japanese children on the streets, I would stop by the school fence and peer into their classrooms. Through the glass windows, which crossed the entire length of the building, I could see the boys engaged in after-school activities. The most fascinating of these was their swordsmanship class. The boys, dressed like little samurai, stood in two lines facing each other, each boy holding a long bamboo sword. Suddenly the teacher would let out an ear-piercing command. The boys in one line would answer with a bloodcurdling scream and lift the swords over their heads. Then with another command they would lunge forward, slashing their swords down. Now, they would step back and resume their pose. At the next command of the teacher, the boys in the opposing line took their turn, screaming, lunging, and slashing. With deadly seriousness, they would repeat this maneuver over and over again. The deafening screams, it seemed, were intended for developing their lung power even more than the muscle power so that should the enemy not be frightened by the sword, he would certainly be terrified by the scream.

The dire consequences of close contact with the Japanese were revealed to me one day by surprise. When I was eight years old, I accompanied my two older sisters and Umma to a grand celebration of my uncle's birthday. As usual, Papa was away from home visiting his churches in distant provinces. This particular uncle was regarded with great respect; he was the last of the Hyuns to have served in high office for the last Korean king. I learned many years later that he had served either as the minister or vice-minister of education. The entire Hyun family in and around Seoul gathered at his palatial home, the only one of many mansions my ancestors had built in Seoul which was still occupied by a Hyun family. At this gathering of the clan, I met all the uncles and aunts and a horde of cousins. All the ladies would be busy scurrying in and out of the huge kitchen, carrying bottles of warm rice wine and freshly broiled meats and fish to the elders. Every now and then, I would be handed a piece of meat or fish. How delectable they were!

While playing with the children, I accidentally discovered an inner gate that was padlocked. When I tried to pry it open, the other children became frightened and ran away. How strange, I thought. The gate led to a rear house, but why the padlock? Filled with curiosity, I pulled Umma aside and asked, "Umma, who lives in the rear house and why is the little gate padlocked?"

"Go and play, Pedro-ya." Umma ignored my question and then changed the subject by saying, "You will have your dinner as soon as the elders have finished." I became more interested in the mystery of the padlocked gate than in the dinner. By nagging the older boys and huddling with them away from the elders, I managed to piece together the terrible tale. My uncle's oldest son had gone to Japan to study and when he had finished school, he returned home with a Japanese wife. Uncle tried to hide this disgrace by installing them in the little rear house. In time, they had two children, a boy and a girl. "Half-breeds!" the children would whisper. "They are not permitted to come to the main house when there are guests." The Japanese wife was allowed to work in the kitchen, cooking and washing dishes. She also did the laundry, and when there were no visitors, she was even allowed to serve at my uncle's dinner table. But on such an occasion as this uncle's birthday celebration, the entire family, including the two children, would be confined to the rear house and the little gate padlocked.

Umma's constant warning about the Japanese, "the vicious natures behind their ingratiating manners and bows," was revealed to me as stark reality on a fine summer day. I was returning home from Sunday School together with my two older sisters, Alice and Elizabeth. (I secretly preferred their Korean names, Mi-Ok, meaning Beautiful Jade, and Young-Ok, Glowing-Jade.) On our way home, the shortest route took us past a Japanese settlement. To avoid it, we would take the longer way around which was almost twice as far. On this warm summer noon, we decided to risk it and go past the cluster of Japanese houses. From a distance, we saw the Japanese children playing in the street. In trepidation, we walked cautiously on the opposite side. Then it happened. One of them barked a command and I saw a huge police dog leap at us. "Umma! Umma!" my sisters screamed, and I ran for my life. Not hearing my sisters, though, I halted and looked back. They were in the ditch, struggling desperately to get away from the mauling dog. I could neither go to their rescue nor run away. The Japanese children were surrounding them, clapping, jumping, and yelling. *"Sa ram sal-yee sai yo!"* I began to scream. *"Sa ram sal-yee sai yo!* Save my life! Save my life!"* Startled, the little devils turned and stared at me. I kept screaming with more and more terror, hoping someone would hear and come to our aid. But it was Sunday and there were no passersby—and surely no Koreans near a Japanese settlement. But my relentless screams had their effect, for the Japanese children took their dog and ran into their homes. Only then did I dare start toward my sisters. They crawled out of the ditch, their hair disheveled, their faces and arms bleeding from the scratches of the dog. We ran home and when Umma opened the gate, all three of us clung to her and broke into uncontrollable sobs.

Fortunately, sometimes a growing child is blessed with a short memory. A year after the attack of the Japanese dog, I accompanied the grown-ups to visit the new Japanese town called Jin Go Gai, "Wet Hill." It lay at the foot of Nam San, the South Mountain which overlooked the entire city of Seoul. Trembling, I held onto the hand of one of the men and as we walked through the street crowded with Japanese men, women, and children. "Be brave," I told myself. "Don't let them know that you are afraid." On this occasion, which was for me a daring excursion, I saw and learned much. All the shops had large windows behind which goods of all kinds were displayed, clothes, dishes, pictures, and plants. I was fascinated by the endless miniatures: tiny screens, tiny dolls, and tiny shrines. I understood why the Koreans called the Japanese the "Little Island People." I also discovered that they were lovers of books. The bookstores were filled with people, all standing around the stalls and reading. I learned that it was the Japanese custom to allow anyone to come into the bookstore, pick out any book they wished, and read.

"What are they all reading?" I asked the elders. "Novels, mostly," I was told. "Some of them may be studying textbooks, but mostly novels." I didn't know what a novel was, for I had never read one.

As a reward for my "mature" behavior, the grown-ups took me

CHAPTER 6

to Jin Go Gai once again, this time at night. Umma gave us her permission. The same street at night was yet another world. All the shops were brightly lit and everything in the stores sparkled and dazzled. The Japanese men and women, dressed in colorful kimonos, strolled, chattering and laughing gaily. We stopped before a Japanese theatre. Long, narrow flags and inscriptions fluttered from tall bamboo poles. We examined the big posters of the actors; all looked serious and fierce. After some debate among the grown-ups, they purchased tickets and we went in. We climbed up to the balcony and sat on the straw mattress. The theatre was filled; the people buzzed excitedly and the vendors cried, "Hot tea! Sweet cakes! . . ." Suddenly the lights dimmed and the entire theatre became hushed. From behind the stage came loud beats of two wooden blocks, *clack, clack, clack.* Then came the rumble of a drum, *boom, boom, boom.* As the beats grew louder and faster, another drum joined in sharp, impatient beats. The curtain parted slowly.

A samurai in elegant costume stood at the center of the stage. He carried a sword at his left side and a short dagger at his right. He strutted a few steps and began to speak. His speech was more like singing or chanting; his voice was deeply guttural and cracked like any self-respecting samurai's voice should be. He moved toward the audience. By his deliberate movements and menacing gestures, I guessed his mood to be highly indignant and understood that he was not to be trifled with. At the end of the speech, he took his stance with feet apart and facing offstage, but his head turned toward the audience in defiance. Now the wood blocks and the drums beat out a new rhythm, more deliberate and sedate. Another samurai appeared onstage; his costume was subdued and somber, and the makeup on his face, very severe. His manners and gestures, however, were no less indignant and his voice no less cracked and harsh. He, too, sang his speech with gestures, and at the end he took his stance opposite the other samurai, turning his head toward the audience as though begging for approval and sympathy. The two samurai then chanted their speeches alternately, and at times simultaneously, with accompanying swordplay and gestures.

Then a piercing, shrill voice was heard. The two samurai froze in their tracks. The inner curtain parted slowly, revealing a stunning female figure. She wore a wispy kimono with bright flower patterns and a golden bow around her waist. Her hair was dressed in the shape of a winged castle. As she spoke in a thin falsetto, she moved in small, weaving steps. Highly excited, the two samurai drew their swords ready to charge. The head of one of the samurai was about to fall. At this crucial moment, the wispy lady tottered over to the samurai on her left, swooned, and fainted. The samurai caught the lady with one arm and shouted a triumphant cry. The other samurai bowed, dropped his head, replaced his sword in its sheath, and staggered off chanting in a most tragic voice and cadence. The curtain closed to the beat of *clack, clack, clack* and *boom, boom, boom.*

I came out of the theatre deeply moved; my mind was in a strange turmoil. The same treacherous, vicious people—how could they create such a noble and beautiful drama? And all those people in the bookstore, how avidly they read! My condemnation of the Japanese people was softening considerably. Such charitable feelings, however, were dispelled soon afterward when the grown-ups took me to another section of the Japanese town. Here, there were no shops. Instead there were only two-story wooden houses with little balconies overlooking the street. From these balconies came soft, sweet voices.

"Irat sai! Hai, irat sai! Come in! Please come in." I looked up and saw young Japanese girls wearing bright kimonos and their faces heavily made up. I asked the grown-ups who they were and whom they were calling. "They are calling for you," they told me teasingly and burst out laughing. I didn't quite understand why they were laughing, but I knew that I was the subject of the joke, and I pretended to be angry.

We walked past more of those two-story houses and saw more pretty young girls whispering, *"Irat sai! Hai, irat sai!"* The grown-ups stopped and engaged in a whispered conversation after which one of the men disappeared into the house. The rest of us walked on to a little park and sat on a bench. The men carried on a most animated conversation. I couldn't understand the nature of the pleasantry, but I knew it had to do with the man who disappeared into the house. Then they turned to me and one of them said, "Next year, for sure, we will take you into the house so that you can meet one of those pretty Japanese girls."

CHAPTER 6

"No, no! I don't want to go in there! I don't want to go in there!" But even as I was protesting so vehemently, for some unknown reason I felt my heart pounding. After a while, the errant friend returned and joined us. Everybody pounded his back lustily with guffaws and exclamations. As I watched the scene, my recently gained feeling of affinity for the Japanese people quickly faded away.

The final blow in regard to the Japanese people fell on me literally with a whiplash. I was thirteen years old, finishing my last year in the public elementary school. In contrast to the private school I had attended, all the teachers there, including the principal, were Japanese. Moreover, while in the private school they taught a few Korean subjects such as history and literature and in the Korean language, in the public school nothing relating to Korea was taught and all the classes were conducted in Japanese. Nevertheless, I had transferred to the public school for two important reasons. First, Father had terminated his ministry at the Jung Dong First Methodist Church and became the director of all the Methodist Sunday Schools throughout Korea. So we had to move out of the minister's home and into a new house which was conveniently located next to a public school. Secondly, to enter the high school we had to pass the examination in Japanese. For this privilege we were forced to attend the public school and endure the daily humiliation heaped upon us.

In the morning, before we went to the classes, we had to assemble in the yard in military formation according to our grades. The principal, wearing a black uniform with gold buttons in the front and a sword at his side, stood at the top of the steps facing us. The teachers, also in black uniform, stood at either side of him. The principal, in his trained samurai voice, would scream out the command *"Kyo tsu geee! Attenn-tion!"* We stiffened our bodies and looked serious. One of the teachers would then step forward and lead us in the Japanese national anthem: *"Gi mi ga-a yo-o wa. . . ."* We were expected to follow him and sing with all our strength. No one knew that every morning I spat out those words of endearment for the emperor of Japan with all my contempt. Another command from the principal, and we would turn and face east in the direction of the rising sun. Then, another scream. We would bend over and hold the reverent pose until the final command to straighten ourselves. Only when this ceremony was over would we march to our classes.

THE JAPANESE

My shaky regard for the Japanese met its final blow on March 4, 1919. The initial wave of demonstrations for Korean independence had been crushed. An edict of the emperor was promulgated which was then printed on big posters and displayed throughout the entire city on the walls, gates, doors, and windows of every public building. No Korean could escape the emperor's message. The imposing seal of the emperor at the bottom of the poster attested to its authenticity and further intimidated all onlookers. One such poster was pinned to the wooden gate of my school. I walked by and stopped to read.

"You miserable Koreans, listen! Listen to your great and magnanimous Emperor." It listed all the kind and generous acts of the emperor for Korea. Infuriated by the insult, I read on.

"Impress your miserable Korean heads with this sacred edict. Hereafter, it shall be unlawful:

- To assemble in public or private in a group of more than three persons.
- To express any ideas critical of the Emperor and his officers.
- To write, print, or distribute any words detrimental to the Emperor or to his government in Korea.
- To disregard, to conspire to disregard, or to obstruct the enforcement of this sacred edict.
- All violators of this edict shall be arrested, imprisoned, and punished."

I stood there for a moment feeling numb and hopeless. Then, for some reason, I became interested in the shiny thumbtacks at the corners of the poster which held it to the wooden gate. I looked about and saw no one. I pried off one of the tacks at the bottom, then another. The poster loosened and began to flap in the wind. Just as I was reaching for the tack on the top, I heard the hoarse voice of a samurai.

"Baka! Baka! Baka!"

Baka is a catch-all Japanese cussword which, depending on the situation, can mean good-for-nothing, a fool, an idiot, or a bastard. I turned and saw a Japanese man running toward me with his arms flailing, his face contorted, seemingly ready to kill me. Away I flew, the Japanese man in pursuit.

"Stop! *Baka,* stop! Catch that *baka!* Somebody! Catch that *baka!*"

67

The mad screams grew louder and I could tell the would-be killer was gaining on me. The frightening thought of being killed by a Japanese gave me a new spurt of strength and speed. At last, the screams and the sound of running feet grew fainter, but I never stopped; I kept running until I couldn't hear any sound of the pursuer. I turned into an alley and ran farther and farther away from home. I was afraid the enraged man might be lurking near my house, waiting for me.

I waited what seemed like hours before I approached home by a roundabout way. Umma looked at me suspiciously and asked where I had been.

"Just outside, playing," I fibbed.

"Your school principal wants you to come and see him right away." Umma seemed agitated. I was puzzled. The principal in school? I couldn't understand. The school had closed for the day long ago.

"I'll see him tomorrow," I said to Umma.

"No, Pedro-ya, you'd better go right now. The janitor was here with the message, and the Sensei, the teacher, will be waiting for you." With great trepidation, I walked out of our rear gate which led to the school building. I stood before the principal's office and announced myself, "*Hai,* Sensei. Yes sir, teacher." The door opened and I saw the tall, slim figure of the principal. I was surprised to see him fully dressed in his black uniform including the sword at his side.

"Come here," he commanded and shut the door behind me.

"What were you doing in front of the school gate?" he asked.

"When, sir?" I asked innocently.

"Just now!" he jumped up. "Just a little while ago!"

"Yes, sir. I was playing."

"Playing?" He seemed on the verge of losing control of himself. "Playing? Playing with the emperor's proclamation? *Baka!*" Then I understood. The madman who failed to catch me had come to the school and reported that I had been tearing down the sacred poster.

"I just wanted to take a thumbtack," I said meekly.

"Thumbtack! Thumbtack!" The screaming was becoming unbearable. "You meant to destroy the emperor's proclamation!" I had no further explanation and remained silent. Infuriated, the principal shouted again.

"Speak! *Baka,* speak! Who told you to do it?"

Silence.

"You miserable Korean *baka!* Confess! Are you guilty? Who told you to do it?"

Silence.

He jumped up and dashed outside. In a flash, he returned holding a handful of long, dried willow reeds, I guessed, broken off the janitor's broom.

"Roll up your pants, *baka!*"

The principal was preparing me for the traditional Korean punishment for children: lashes on the bare legs. But a Korean used only one piece of reed, not a whole bundle. When the first lash whistled down on my legs, I knew it was not a Korean punishment. With the bundle of reeds, he whipped me with all his strength. I cringed but remained erect. With each blow, the principal barked.

"Speak! Speak! Speak!"

The more he whipped, the more I gritted my teeth and remained silent. The principal then lost all control. He kept whipping without stop, and, not satisfied, he began hitting me all over my body. I covered my head and he whipped my hands. He was a madman. He kept it up until he became exhausted. Finally he threw down the shredded reeds and began slapping me with his hands.

"*Baka!* You miserable Korean *baka!* Get out! Get out!" I limped away in slow painful steps.

It was almost dark when I got home. Umma rushed to me and looked at my swollen face. "Oh, my God! What happened? What happened?"

"He gave me a whipping for taking the thumbtacks off the poster."

"Let me see your legs." I turned and rolled up my pants.

"Oh, my God!" Umma shrieked. My sisters ran in and covered their faces at the gory sight and began to cry.

"A thumbtack! And he gave you such a beating!" Sister Alice dashed out to the kitchen and returned with a pan full of warm water. Umma sprinkled some salt over the water, stirred it, and began to dab and wash my legs with a cloth. I had so steeled myself during the beating, I couldn't even feel the sting of saltwater on the wounds.

"Oh, my God! Oh, my God!" Umma kept moaning as she gently washed my legs. "Oh, my God! Your legs are covered with blood!" I turned and put my hand on her shoulder.

"Umma! Umma!" I told her with pride in my voice, "the Japanese principal beat me until he got tired. But Umma, through the whole beating I didn't cry." When I finished telling her how contemptuous and brave I was, I broke down and cried my heart out.

7

THE FLIGHT TO CHINA

IT WAS TIME for our family to leave Korea, perhaps never to return. But we would no longer be hounded by the Japanese police and we would leave behind the humiliation of begging for food from day to day. And we would find Papa in China; the chances of his return to Korea had become more and more remote. So our departure in the night to an unknown land was a desperate escape, a cruel exile, and a search for our father.

I have only sketchy memories of our hasty departure from Seoul. But some things still stand out sharply: scenes and images that persist in my mind's eye. I know it was in the fall because there were leaves on the ground beneath the poplar trees which line the streets of Seoul. I also remember our mother, Umma, dressing us in padded cotton clothes for the chilly evening air. I do not remember exactly how we got to the South Gate railway station, however. I know we didn't ride in rickshaws, for that would have been too expensive and our guide, Uncle Lee, wouldn't have allowed it even if we could have afforded it. Uncle Lee was from Kaesong and the people of Kaesong were known for their frugality. If anyone wished to save money in any undertaking, the saying was: "Just ask someone from Kaesong."

We must all have walked to the station, as usual, the older ones carrying the younger ones on their backs. But the bundles! How did they get to the station? Those bundles might have appeared pitifully ordinary, but they carried the sum total of our family treasures: our clothes, shoes and sandals, a box containing colored ribbons for Umma's and my sisters' hair, a miniature chest of drawers with all the silver and gold ornaments for the ladies and other items which Umma could not part with, such as family photographs. And, of course, special bundles of all kinds of food for the long journey. We did leave behind all of our family brassware which included the precious dishes and bowls for each of us that were handed down for generations and worn thin from use. Also sadly left behind were the family silver spoons and chopsticks of various sizes for every member and all the kitchen things—all the jars, pots and pans, and earthenware with the delicious *kim-chee* still left in them. But for me, the saddest things to leave were the scrolls and paintings which hung on the walls ever since I could remember, especially the six-leaf lacquer screen with carved pictures that always stood in our sleeping room. The graceful cranes, the romping horses, the sleeping lions, all carved in the screen panels, and the wondrous world of mountains, forests, and rivers painted on the scrolls with such dashes and flourishes—they harbored all my childhood dreams: mysterious journeys, inspiring hopes, secret plans. Today I can close my eyes and see them still.

But how strange! Not one of the people who had received these family treasures as parting gifts came to the station to see us leave. Only a handful of friends accompanied us to the station, each carrying a bundle, wishing us a safe journey. Among them was the faithful deacon of Father's church, Mr. Chung, whose body had been shattered in prison by the Japanese. As the train slowly moved out of the station, I complained to Umma.

"How is it that none of our relatives came to the station?" I asked bitterly. "And those good friends who took all our family treasures, none of them showed up. Didn't they know we were leaving Korea for good and going to a foreign country to live?"

"Pedro-ya," Umma whispered in her comforting voice, "you must understand. They are all afraid of the Japanese police. They didn't want to be seen with us because then the police would go after them after we leave."

The inside of the train was bare except for two long wooden benches which ran the whole length of the train on either side. Some of our smaller bundles were put on the overhead rack and the rest on the floor. We settled down in a corner and all of us were silent for a long time; we could not believe what was happening to us. I leaned against the window and stared at the disappearing city, then the Han River which we crossed over a steel bridge, and soon the countryside with patches of rice fields and clusters of thatched-roof farmhouses. The sun began to set and soon there was nothing but darkness. When would we see it all again? Our mood was made even sadder by the unrelenting shakes and jolts and the cry of the wheels grinding over the rail.

Sensing the family sinking into a mood of self-pity, Umma wisely announced it was time for supper. She opened one of the bundles and took out a handsome box. She handed each of us, except the babies, a lacquered bowl and a pair of matching chopsticks. She filled our bowls with *bee-bim-bap,* the traditional Korean dish made of rice mixed with bits of marinated meat, bean sprouts, pickled radish, and seasoned with soy sauce and sesame oil. Somehow, eating on a moving train made it more tasty, fun, and delicious, and when I asked for a second helping, Umma didn't admonish me as usual for eating too fast. Uncle Lee was so conscious of saving money, he refused to have a second helping! By the time we finished our first meal on the train, we must have left our home city of Seoul far behind. Other people, I noticed, were also having their supper, some out of bowls, some out of little bamboo baskets, and others, balls of rice wrapped in newspaper. They all had one thing in common: *kim-chee* and the fumes of the fermented garlic permeated throughout the car, attesting it was truly a Korean train!

Sister Alice gathered all the empty bowls and chopsticks and put them back in the bundle. She would have to wait for the next stop to have them washed, a ritual she was to follow for the rest of the journey. Uncle Lee then untied our bedding and spread the cotton mattresses on the floor. First, Umma laid baby Mary down; she was barely a year old and cried constantly protesting the strange surroundings. But Umma, our tiny mother with an inexhaustible supply of milk, pacified the baby. Next David, age three, took his place on the mattress, his eyes darting and noting everything; he was a very watchful child. A little space was left between them for Umma to lie down whenever she could. Next to David, Joshua, age four, lay down and immediately fell asleep.

CHAPTER 7

Joshua was called the resurrected one by everyone who knew him. We were living in the minister's home at Jung Dong First Methodist Church when it happened. The newborn baby, Joshua, was not yet a year old when one summer day he fell seriously ill with a high fever which would not subside even with the strongest herb medicine Umma could find. After several days of suffering, our little baby brother died. He had hardly lived long enough to be counted as a member of the family, and now he was dead. Umma put the still body of infant Joshua in an empty room for burial the next day. Friends from the church gathered in the living room and kept vigil. They sang hymns, offered prayers, and consoled Umma for the sudden sad loss. They parted late in the evening, to return the following day to attend the funeral. At dawn the next day, into the room where we were sleeping dashed Umma clutching the little bundle of Joshua.

"He is alive! He is alive!" Umma was beside herself with joy. "He is breathing! He is alive! He is breathing!" Umma bared her breast and offered it to the baby. We gathered around her and watched the baby suckling with all his might. We jumped up and down and clapped our hands.

"Joshua! Joshua! Joshua!" We all yelled, "You are alive! You are alive!" When the friends arrived for the expected furneral, Umma told them the incredible story. She'd been unable to sleep all through the night and at daybreak had gone weeping to the empty room where the dead baby lay. She lifted the cotton veil to look at the baby once more. The baby's eyes were open and blinking. She leaned over and felt the baby's body. It was warm. That's when she lifted him and ran into our sleeping room screaming, "He is alive! He is alive!"

Joshua, the resurrected one; he truly came back from the dead. And as if to prove it had really happened, at the age of three Joshua "died" again. This time Umma was especially careful and made certain of his death before taking the body to an empty room. She then made all the necessary arrangements for burial the next day. But at daybreak, drawn by an irresistible desire, Umma got out of bed and went to see her child who had died for the second time. And there he was—with his eyes wide open and smiling at Umma. She snatched him and brought him back to the warm room. This time there was no screaming, only acceptance and gratitude. And now here was Joshua with all of us, with his brothers and sisters, with Umma and Uncle Lee, sleeping so soundly in the noisy, rattling train bound for unknown far-off places.

Next Paul, age seven, lay down opposite the little ones, his feet touching theirs. Paul was a child of few words. His responses were always brief and direct: "No, I don't want it." "Yes, I like it." His gifts and talents and thoughts were always self-contained, undisturbed by anything around him. Next to Paul lay Soon-Ok, "Gentle Jade." I don't know why, of all the eight children, she was never given either a biblical or a Western name. She was my favorite, not out of pity because she was crippled but because she was the wittiest. She always saw the funny side of everything and made everybody laugh. What a pity that she'd become a hunchback at age six. Her condition grew increasingly severe as she got older and now we had to carry her everywhere we went.

It had happened while visiting our grandparents. Apparently she fell on a huge block of granite which served as a stepping stone to the open living room. No one ever discovered how it had happened, but it seemed that she had fallen on it backwards and broke her back. Am-Bang Grandmother was so frightened that she never mentioned it to Umma, and Soon-Ok too kept her word and never told anyone about the fall. Indeed, the injury was not discovered until almost a year later when the pain became increasingly worse. Umma took her to a doctor who discovered a little protrusion in her spine. It was too late to do anything for her, Umma was told. While confined to bed most of the time, she would study all my schoolbooks and manage to keep her class standing with me. In fact, she would do a lot of my homework, especially arithmetic and composition—another reason, of course, why she was my favorite sister.

Finally, it was my turn to lie down. I kept all my clothes on except the sandals and the cotton padded Korean stockings. Among the children, I was the emotional one, the impetuous one; my head was filled with new fancies and ideas and I was always restless. I usually spent my energy by visiting Ewha College, the first women's college in Korea, which was located next to Father's church. It was so much fun there—to burst into the girls' dormitory and see them squeal and run, or to raid the garden where Mrs. Tuttle, the principal, raised and guarded her precious American fruits and vegetables. After each escapade, the reproaches were always hurled at my two sisters, Alice and Elizabeth, who were attending the middle school there. In turn, they would report it to Umma with painful cries, "Umma, Pedro did it again!" Sympathetic but not unduly excited over such regular occurrences, Umma would only ask, "Well, what did he do this time?"

But no prank of mine reached the height of scandal I achieved on one summer day. It was on a hot Sunday afternoon, so hot that no one was to be seen around the college, my favorite playground. I gathered several boys, faithful followers of mine, and went there to explore. After a futile search for anything that might be fun, we came upon the well in back of Mrs. Tuttle's house. In Korean, her name, Tuttle, meant "shake" and she happened to possess an enormous bosom that shook up and down as she walked. By watching the intensity of the shake, we could tell what kind of mood she was in. On this hot day, I discovered a piece of string that was tied to the rack on top of the well. It went down all the way to the bottom of the well and was tied to a large bottle submerged in the cool water. I pulled the bottle up and found it filled with some brown liquid. I untied it, and clutching the bottle, we stole away to our secret hideaway.

Triumphantly, I opened the bottle and tasted its contents. I was disappointed; it was tasteless and I spat it out. I passed the bottle around and asked my friends to taste it. Each performed the same ceremony: swallow and spit.

"What is it?" I asked.

"It's tasteless!" All agreed.

"But what is it?" I asked again.

"Tastes like tea," someone suggested.

I took another swallow, winced, and spat it out. "You are right," I said, "it is tea. But why did 'Shake Shake' put the tea in a bottle and drop it in the well?" No one could offer any explanation. An idea flashed through my head. I emptied the bottle and refilled it by peeing in it. The bottle was passed around for each one's contribution until it was full again. The color was amazingly similar to the tea we had just disposed of. My friends were too afraid to return, so I went back alone and tied the bottle at the end of the string and dropped it into the well. As far as I was concerned, that was the end of the fun with the mysterious bottle of tea.

THE FLIGHT TO CHINA

The following Sunday morning, I went to the Sunday School as usual which was held in the Ewha College auditorium. To my surprise, I saw Mrs. Tuttle sitting on the platform along with the Korean principal, the frail and meek Mr. Chung. The expression on Mrs. Tuttle's face was ominous; even worse, her arms crossed in front, holding up her bosom, signified serious business. I turned to my cohorts and passed the signal: "Not a word. Silence at all cost." Dispensing with the usual singing and opening prayer, Mr. Chung stepped forward and faced us.

He cleared his throat several times and said, "Something terrible happened last Sunday afternoon." He cleared his throat again and said, "Who did it? We want to know who did it." Acting surprised, I turned to my friends and said in a loud whisper for everyone to hear, "Who did what? Eh? Do you know who did what?" Now Mrs. Tuttle stood up and shook and shook her way to the edge of the platform. Her voice also shook as she spoke in her odd Korean which sounded like a pumpkin rolling down a hill, but quite understandable.

"Who . . . did . . . it?" she said slowly. "I . . . want . . . to know . . . who . . . did it." When she was greeted with a long silence, she threatened us, "I . . . will stay here . . . and not go away . . . until I find out . . . who did it." All the girls sitting across the aisle from the boys turned and stared at me. I was the picture of innocence. I don't remember how long the awkward moment lasted, but we were finally dismissed without singing and without any concluding prayer. It was the shortest Sunday School session of my life. I have never stopped feeling the pangs of conscience when I recall that hot Sunday afternoon and the bottle of tea in the well. I still laugh too!

Now all the people in the train were preparing to go to sleep. Except for a few, they were poorly dressed. I guessed they were farmers returning home after the sale of their products in Seoul. Most of them wore pantaloons and jackets with a variety of patches on them. There were also a couple of country scholars whose distinguishing feature was the long hair tied into short knobs on the top of their heads. And over the knobs they wore tall, stiff hats made of black horsehair. These hats would be carefully removed and placed safely beside them before they lay down to sleep. Gradually, all the passengers settled in clusters on the bench or on the floor and went to sleep.

I took my place on the floor next to Soon-Ok. I could see my sister Elizabeth stretched out on the bench using one of the bundles as a backrest. All of the children called our sister Elizabeth "The Hider." She hid everything that belonged to her. They were her treasures: bits of cloth of all colors left over from Umma's sewing, threads and buttons, but the most precious, as far as I could see, were the candies and nuts she had received from Umma as her share. She wouldn't eat them all at once like the rest of us; she would save and hide them with the rest of her treasures. But I would always manage to find them and steal them. I would dash out of the house, hide behind a corner, and eat them as fast as I could. Then I would have to face the usual retribution.

"Umma! Umma! Umma!" Sister Elizabeth would cry her heart out. "Pedro again! Pedro again!"

"What now?" Umma wasn't too excited.

"He stole all my candies and nuts." She sobbed even more loudly. Her heartrending cry would really touch me and I would feel truly sorry, but there was nothing I could do. Besides, why didn't she eat them when she had them, or hide them where I couldn't find them?

The *knock, knock, knock* and *rattle, rattle, rattle* of the train now became a steady drone.

Before I fell asleep, I glanced at Sister Alice, the oldest one, lying down on the bench with a bundle for her head and turning her back to us. Yes, the heavy burden of taking care of us seven younger ones was now over; she could turn her back and forget us for the night. Sister Alice was our "Second Umma." She was also the beautiful one: angular face, pointed chin, and large, round limpid eyes. Her willowy body moved gracefully no matter how hurried she was. She would always get up before everyone else and cook our breakfast, prepare our school lunch, and then perform the daily chore of coaxing Sister Elizabeth to hurry because Elizabeth hated to go to school and delayed it as long as she could. When she came home after school, Sister Alice's work would really begin: washing and mending clothes and cooking dinner. Of course, Umma was always there, too, but without Sister Alice the housework would never be done. Sister Alice was also my booster and mentor; I always went to her for comfort in times of doubt and distress. I could depend on obtaining from her what I could not get from Umma—unquestioning support. The drone of the train became fainter and fainter. . . . I began to dream of all that I was leaving behind . . .

my friends . . . Am-Bang Grandmother and Grandfather whom I may never see again . . . all . . . all . . . all were fading away . . . all except the sharp image of the Japanese teacher who had given me such a terrible beating. . . .

"Pyongyang! Pyongyang! Pyongyang Station!" I thought I had been sleeping only for a short while, but the conductor's cry startled me. The call of the Pyongyang Station had a magical ring. I remembered from my earliest childhood listening to the elders talking about Pyongyang: the Pyongyang people, Pyongyang foods, Pyongyang customs, and so on. I was led to believe that Pyongyang Saram, meaning Pyongyang people, were almost like foreigners. Their temperament and customs were utterly different from those of southern Korea, especially the people of Seoul. The elders always spoke of them maliciously and disparagingly.

It wasn't until many years later that I learned of the deep roots of mistrust and antagonism between the Pyongyang and the Seoul people. The oldest Korean kingdom was known as Koguryo. It was established about the year 37 B.C. and flourished until A.D. 927. The kingdom encompassed not only the northern portion of the Korean peninsula but also most of Manchuria. Its proud capital was Pyongyang. When this mighty kingdom was overthrown and the Koryu kingdom established, the capital was moved from Pyongyang to Kaesong in the south. All "northerners" were banished from official positions and relegated to the lowest social status. Thus the seeds of segregation and hatred were planted and their poisonous fruits visited upon all their children a thousand years later.

"Pyongyang! Pyongyang! Pyongyang!" My heart throbbing with excitement, I got up and looked out the window. The day was just dawning; I could only see the dim outline of the station building, which didn't seem very impressive. When the train stopped, there was a frantic movement of people getting on and off. I noticed the people were dressed somewhat differently: farmers in bulky clothes with white cotton leggings and women with wide white bands tied around their hair. When the train began to move, I was glued to the window trying to see every bit of the legendary city. There wasn't much to see; the train kept passing by a mass of little low houses of the poor working people. Then suddenly we left the hovels behind and were crossing a wide river. It must have been the great Taedong River. On the banks and on the hillside, overlooking the river, there were old twisted pines and at the crest I could see the outline of a pagoda and a temple. My ancestors had sailed this river, had prayed in that temple, and had played in that pagoda. Oh, how I wished I could have gotten off the train and seen those landmarks of Korean history!

Along with the rest of the waking passengers, one by one, we all woke up: first Sister Alice, then Umma, and then all the young ones. Baby Mary gave out a piercing morning cry, and Umma pacified her with her breast. After that, the first chore was to prepare breakfast for everyone. Like magic, Umma pulled an earthen pot out of a bundle, and with a wooden ladle she dished out *jook* into little lacquered bowls for everyone. It was still warm and delicious. *Jook* is a special Korean breakfast dish made by boiling the cooked rice in a chicken or beef broth for a long time until the rice becomes a smooth gruel very tasty and very easy to digest. Of course, it's always served with bits of *kim-chee* on the side. Now the train passed through rugged, mountainous country. It would come out of one dense pine forest only to enter another. It sped over little streams and rivers and then wound around another mountainside. Time passed; it was almost noon.

"Sin Eu-ju! Sin Eu-ju! Sin Eu-ju Station!" The conductor's call set all the people on the train astir with a sudden flurry of movement. It was the last stop on Korean soil. We would now have to cross the gigantic Ap-Nok, the Yalu River, to reach China.

This last stop on Korean soil had a special portent for the Hyun family. Would the Japanese police accept the permit we had obtained in Seoul and let us pass through, or would they reject it on some pretext and force us to return to Seoul? Uncle Lee appeared calm enough and told Umma that he would go to the police station and obtain the necessary approval. But Umma was agitated and insisted that she accompany him. When they left the train, we huddled around Sister Alice for protection. I asked her if she thought the Japanese police would make us go back. She hushed me and said that Umma would take care of the police. At last I saw Umma and Uncle Lee returning; they both seemed jubilant. We surrounded them and asked, "Can we go? Can we go?"

"Yes, yes, yes," Umma patted us, "of course, of course, we can go."

"Ajumu-nim, honorable aunt," Uncle Lee addressed Umma, "that was a stroke of inspiration. What made you think of the name of the American missionary working in the Japanese church?"

"Because," Umma answered, "I supposed his name would be known to Japanese police all over Korea."

"Well," Uncle Lee mused, "we might have gotten through anyway. But your mentioning the missionary's name to the police chief certainly worked like magic."

The Yalu River was as majestic as it was turbulent. I walked to the end of the train and watched the river flow under the immense steel bridge. It was a sad but dramatic farewell to Korea. It was a long crossing and when we reached land at the other end, it was Fung-Ten, China. Yes, we were in China!

The first thing that made me conscious of being in a foreign land was the sound of the language the people spoke. It wasn't just the difference in the sounds, but in the intensity, the intonation, and the emotion of the sound. In vain, I tried to understand some of their words, any words. Fortunately, Uncle Lee understood and spoke Chinese. Soon, he'd arranged our transportation to a hotel as we had an overnight wait for the train which would take us across Manchuria to the city of Tientsin. That next journey, we were told, would take two nights and three days. Uncle Lee hailed several man-drawn, one-wheel carts. A large wheel was fixed in the center with wide seats built on either side of the wheel for loading passengers and goods. Wooden guards kept the wheel away from the loads. The cart was triangular with the pointed end at the front and the wider part, with a handle on either side, at the rear.

The coolie, the lowest-class laborer, would slip the ends of a strong strap around the cart handles and then loop it behind his neck and around the shoulders. He could then lift the load with his whole body and push it and steer it with his hands. Now a parade of these carts, carrying Umma and Uncle Lee and us eight children, as well as the bundles, bedding, and boxes, seemed to arouse quite an interest among the passersby and not a few loud but incomprehensible comments. I didn't mind; I was enjoying their sights, the sights of so many Chinese people all engaged in some activity, all crying, yelling, and hawking, all selling and buying something. It seemed like a carnival.

Our first "hotel" in China was a great disappointment. It turned out to be an overnight sleeping place for the cart and rickshaw pullers; it was Uncle Lee's idea of finding shelter for the night at the cheapest possible cost. The poor coolies' "hotel" consisted of one large mud-floored room with a stack of wooden benches against the wall. Fortunately, there was a small inner room which was heated by burning wood under the upraised floor, much as in the Korean house. Into this tiny but secluded room, Umma corralled all my sisters and younger brothers. Uncle Lee, Brother Paul, and I were to sleep on benches in the mud-floored dormitory. Before retiring, Uncle Lee went out and brought a large pot of noodles called *ja-jang mien*. It was plain boiled noodles mixed in a salty, dark bean sauce. Once again, Uncle Lee had found the least expensive food for our supper. But this was our first meal in China and we all ate it with much laughter, teasing Uncle Lee about his Kaesong tightness with money.

"Remember, children," Uncle Lee admonished us, "I have to take you all as far as Shanghai . . . and it will cost a lot of money." It was time to go to sleep. Uncle Lee, Brother Paul, and I left Umma and her brood in the warm room and went to the mud-floored hall. Each of us took a bench, put it on the floor, and lay down on it to sleep. For quite a while, I found it impossible to fall asleep on such a narrow wooden bench. But the day's long, tiring ride, the excitement, and the strain of being in a foreign land all overwhelmed me and I soon closed my eyes.

I was awakened from my deep sleep by the noise of moving benches, loud mumblings, and bursts of laughter. I opened my eyes and looked around. To my amazement, the entire room was filled with men lying on benches; the rows of benches were so close together, some of them were actually touching each other. I guessed there were nearly a hundred men, most of them already asleep, others just getting ready. The stench of these laborers who had pulled rickshaws and carts all day was overwhelming. At that moment, I remembered the scorn with which I used to regard all "Dwei-nom," the deprecating name given to all Chinese immigrants in Korea. "Dwei-nom" literally meant "pig-son." The Chinese immigrants in Korea, with the exception of the few merchants who had shops selling imported goods from China, were farmers who peddled their vegetables to the Koreans.

There were others, however, who were excellent bakers of *ho-duk*, a sweet, round cake the size of a man's palm, made of plain flour dough with a dab of melted brown sugar stuffing. These were baked to order in a clay oven and the Koreans loved to eat them at all hours of the day and night. And now I was in China sleeping with a horde of these "Dwei-nom" as companions!

When I woke again it was dawn and I found the entire room empty as though the coolies had never been there; they couldn't have slept more than a few hours. Uncle Lee, Brother Paul, and I stacked our benches against the wall and joined the family in the inner room. Sister Alice was already up and had fixed our breakfast. Joshua and David were sitting on the floor in a stupor. Sister Soon-Ok, bright-eyed, was full of questions about my night in the mud-floored room. Sister Elizabeth didn't seem to care much about whatever was happening. When we finished our morning meal, Uncle Lee announced another money-saving plan.

"Since we don't have as many bundles as when we started," he said, "we'll hire just one cart to carry all the load, and we will walk to the station." All of us groaned in dismay. "It's really very close by here," Uncle Lee assured us. So, with bundles piled high and tied down, one cart led the way and we followed on foot. Down the street we marched carrying the small bundles and little brothers and sisters on our backs. Uncle Lee was at the head with a bundle over his shoulder. Behind him walked Umma with baby sister tied to her back and with two bundles, one in each hand. Then came Sister Elizabeth carrying Brother David on her back and Sister Alice holding Brother Joshua by one hand and with the other hand holding onto a large bundle over her shoulder. I followed at the end of the line carrying my sister Soon-Ok on my back. This parade of a family in Korean costume must have presented a strange sight. People stopped to stare at us, and we were all tiring because the railway station was not as near as Uncle Lee had led us to believe.

The Chinese Trans-Manchurian train was quite a bit different from the Korean train. It was narrower with short wooden benches across the car and an aisle in the center. The backs of the seats were made to tilt either way, to face forward or backward. By arranging these benches to face each other and filling the space between seats with bundles, we made fairly comfortable beds. Leaving Fung-Ten, the last link with Korea, and traveling through the endless Manchurian plains was like going into another world. For two days and nights, we crossed those plains without seeing any mountains or hills, any woods or rivers; it was an immense deserted world of wind and dust. The only relief from the monotony was the periodic stop at some wayside station, a village or a small town. Whenever we approached these stops, hordes of beggars, men, women, and children, ran after the train shaking their baskets, bowls, whatever they had that could catch the coins tossed out the window. It was a pitiful sight and I noticed very few coins thrown. The beggars took up the chase again when the train left the station. At some stops, I would leave the train and walk about the platform. On the other side of the fence, vendors held out all kinds of food—many kinds of fruits and cakes, chunks of meat, broiled chicken—and cried out at the passengers. At one such stop, I did buy some roasted chestnuts because they were so reminiscent of Korea, but they didn't taste like the Korean chestnuts.

On the morning of the third day, we arrived at Tientsin, a big city directly across from Port Arthur where a great naval battle was fought between Russia and Japan. The station was in the heart of the city, so we had only to walk a short distance to a nearby restaurant for our lunch. It was the first real treat from Uncle Lee, who must have felt a little more at ease with the budget as we neared our destination. We piled our bundles in the cement patio before we were taken into a large room with a huge square table in the center. Both the table and chairs were carved with decorations of dragons and pine trees, and the shiny lacquer gave off a strong but pleasant smell. Uncle Lee gave the orders to the Chinese waiter who soon brought a steaming bowl of soup. The baby broke into a shrill cry again, protesting the strange surroundings. Umma handed the baby to Sister Alice and began to serve us the soup.

I was surprised by the soup's wonderful taste. It was different from any soup I had ever eaten, rich with bits of meat, shredded chicken, crisp vegetables, and chopped roasted nuts. What a great treat after having lived on only rice and *kim-chee* and noodles for three days! All the other dishes served after the soup were equally delicious and exciting. But the dish that lingered in my memory for a long time was the noodles. That common and ordinary food, noodles? Yes, the noodles I ate in the Tientsin restaurant were most extraordinary. As nearly as I can remember, they were the thinnest threads of noodle, gently fried to crispness without losing their chewy texture, and they were covered with a rich, golden sauce with chicken, mushroom, and diced vegetables. Years later, I had the dubious pleasure of opening a restaurant in California where I attempted to reproduce and serve this wondrous noodle dish as a specialty. It always pained me to be told by my American customers, "Pretty good chow mein."

Our energy renewed and our morale boosted by the wonderful meal, we trudged back to the railway station. The new train would take us on the last stops of our long journey: Nanking and then Shanghai. We would have to spend only one more night on the train. But compared to the Manchurian railway, this train was luxurious; the benches were not only wider but contoured and painted. The windows, too, were bigger and cleaner so that we had a clearer view of the scenes outside. As the train moved out of Tientsin, however, all we could see were dirty houses and blackened factories. Still, I thought it was better than the Manchurian plains with their swirling dust. Soon we left the city behind and began to see the welcome sight of hills in the distance. Then for the rest of the day we passed through rich farmland. The fields were dotted with farmhouses, and around each farm the farmers and their family bent over their crop like a still life. Because of the big lunch we had had, and because all the food brought from Korea was gone, we had a meager supper of some cakes we bought at a station stop. The sun had already set, and once again we were enveloped by the dim light overhead and the monotonous drone of the train. We made up our beds and went to sleep; it was my first comfortable night.

Early next morning, the train stopped at Paw-Ku. It was the end of the line; the great Yangtse River blocked any further progress. On the opposite shore was the capital city of Nanking. All the passengers jumped off and ran pell-mell toward the boats tied at the pier. We had to struggle to keep ourselves together and not be swept away by the human wave. With Uncle Lee shouting and screaming in Chinese, we managed to get aboard all together. The boat was already filled with people, some of them sitting on bundles and boxes. The boat was really only a barge, and with the overloaded mass of people and their nondescript belongings, the air was heavy and acrid. It got better, though, as the barge moved out onto the turbulent waters of the Yangtse. I looked back at the railway terminal and pier we had just left. It was my final farewell: to the desolate Manchurian plains, to the bridge over the wild Yalu River, to the old city of Pyongyang, and to all the friendly hills and people of Seoul. From now on I would only look ahead, at the approaching shore and the city of Nanking. Very soon, I would be securely planted on Chinese soil.

We got off the barge safely without losing anyone or anything. There was no time to see the city; we had to hurry and catch the train to Shanghai. If we could get on it, we might arrive in Shanghai before dark. We were fortunate to get on and left the low hills around Nanking and rode through level countryside, not barren and dusty like Manchuria but fertile and green. Streams crisscrossed here and there, and now and then we passed pretty hills with dense woods and pagodas at the top. Umma and all of us children grew anxious as we approached our final destination.

The Shanghai station was an immense place. A steel dome covered the main hall, and there were countless rows of trains, some idle, some puffing steam, some swallowing up passengers and others spitting them out. We squeezed our way through the crowd and past one of the many gates to the main hall. Even this immense hall was crowded, however, and it took all our yelling and pulling to stay together. Finally we reached the street where we were greeted by shouting rickshaw pullers. There were no cheap one-wheel carts here, so directed by Uncle Lee we all climbed on the rickshaws and had to ride through the entire city before we arrived at the place he had chosen.

Riding through the streets of Shanghai was a new experience. I had always believed the city of Seoul was the biggest city in the world, but I discovered that it could be hidden in a corner of Shanghai. Streams of streetcars, automobiles, rickshaws, and bicycles, not to mention crowds of people walking, packed the streets. We passed along a winding river. It was filled with sampans on which I saw people laundering, cooking, and eating. Then we turned into the main thoroughfare called the Bund which skirted the Shanghai harbor. One side of this wide boulevard was lined with tall brick and stone buildings, and on the opposite side, people strolled in a tree-lined park. I tried to capture as much of the fleeting sights and sounds of the throbbing city as possible while the coolie deftly maneuvered the rickshaw through the dense traffic.

The hotel Uncle Lee had selected was in the heart of the "International Settlement." I was to learn later that Shanghai did not legally belong to China but to a group of Western nations. After World War I, Germany lost its concession and the United States relinquished its, all of which became the International Settlement. In its administration, however, it was basically British: British law and British police. The other major sector of Shanghai was the French Concession administered by the French under French law and French police. At the time of our arrival, the Japanese had succeeded in penetrating the International Settlement and winning the cooperation of the British in rooting out Korean revolutionaries. The French, however, refused to let the Japanese operate within their territory. Uncle Lee hustled us into a room in the hotel and lectured to us. "There are Japanese spies everywhere in Shanghai," he said ominously. "Korean revolutionaries have been kidnapped and sent back to Korea." He lowered his voice, "I am going out to look for your father. But I don't want any Japanese spy to follow me, so it may take a long time." Then in a grave tone of voice he said, "Do not leave this room. All of you, wait here until I get back."

"Before you leave," Umma asked of Uncle Lee, "please arrange for a bath for all of us . . . and a little food for the children." Only when Uncle Lee had left and closed the door behind him did we think of his admonition and began to feel a creeping fear. Our mood was broken by the clatter of a workman who brought a huge wooden tub and set it down on the cement floor. Next he brought two kerosene cans filled with steaming hot water. They were hung on each end of a bamboo pole he carried on his shoulders. He poured the hot water into the tub and then added cold water from the faucet. Umma dipped her hand in and nodded her approval, and the workman left us. First, all my sisters took their baths using the towels we had brought from Korea, then Umma and the youngest ones. When Umma called the workman and gestured to him, he understood and changed the water in the tub with fresh hot water. It was now the boys' turn. Rubbing ourselves with soapy towels and pouring bowls of warm water over our bodies helped us to relax and forget our fears of the Japanese spies. Our bodies and spirits revived with new hope.

Uncle Lee returned late at night; the little ones were already asleep. He was excited and jubilant.

"Great luck," he exclaimed. "I found him! I found your father." He said that at first all the Koreans he contacted were suspicious and would not give him any information. "After hours of futile searching," he said, "I finally met a Kaesong woman from my hometown. Oh, what luck that was!" With a big sigh, he continued, "But even she would not believe me until she had checked all my family ties. Then she took me to a place where a group of men blindfolded me and took me to where your father was. He didn't recognize me at first, but when I told him that his family was in Shanghai, he became so excited he could hardly control himself."

"So, what do we do now?" Umma asked eagerly.

"So, now we all go to his place."

"Why didn't he come to meet us?"

"Impossible. Couldn't take the chance. Like all the Korean revolutionaries, he lives in the French Concession where the Japanese have not yet dared to conduct their raids. They even advised against sending any guards to escort the family."

The little ones were lifted out of their sleep and all of us were hustled out of the hotel for a midnight rickshaw ride. The slap, slap, slap of the rickshawmen's bare feet on the pavement accelerated my own heartbeat. Soon we left the bright city lights and entered a wide boulevard that was only dimly lit. The barren limbs of the trees along the street cast eerie shadows and the autumn wind blew the fallen leaves across our path. After what seemed an interminable ride, the rickshaws halted in front of an imposing iron gate. When we were all unloaded, Uncle Lee dashed into the cavernous alley and then dashed back with a group of young men. They picked up all the bundles and the little children. Umma, my sisters, and I followed them.

The cement-paved alleyway ran through the center of a large compound, and narrow passages ran off the alley on either side. In each passage, there was a row of doors indicating a group of separate housing. The compound could easily have contained a hundred units of such housing. We turned off into one of these passages, and after passing several doors, stopped in front of the last one, a little dark red door. As I write this, I see it once again. It was open and we walked in. I saw

Papa standing there in the middle of the room with a broad smile and a glint of tears in his eyes. First, he took baby Sister Mary and Brother David, one in each arm, and hugged them. Everyone stood around and watched them, and when Papa released the two, Joshua and Paul ran to him and took firm possession of his legs. That helped to relieve the tension. Papa grabbed them with his familiar epithet: *"Ee-nom-ah! Ee-nom-ah!* Rascals! Rascals!"

When the laughter subsided, Sister Alice and then Sister Elizabeth stepped in front and offered Papa the traditional Korean bow: slowly sitting down without losing balance and then, with both hands at the side of the ankles, bowing demurely with downcast eyes. Then it was my turn to perform the traditional ceremony: down on the knees, hands held together in front of the forehead, and slowly bowing until the forehead touched the floor. I heard a loud applause. But Umma, where is Umma? She had taken refuge with the crying baby. And Uncle Lee, the dear man who had protected and guided us across the continent of Asia, now stood against the wall in the background with folded arms as if to say, "Now my work is done."

CLACK! CLACK! CLACK!

The sharp sound of a bamboo pipe was coming from somewhere outside. When I asked, they said that it was the signal of the midnight food vendor. Some of the young men ran out and came back with large bowls of steaming *jook,* the rice gruel. We all sat at the big square table and they served us the *jook* with soy sauce and roasted peanuts in separate dishes. This was the first meal in our Shanghai home.

We had hardly finished when someone discovered the little ones had again fallen asleep on the floor. At one end of the living room there was an upraised section which was enclosed on three sides and shielded in front by a flimsy curtain. Sister Soon-Ok would sleep there, Umma decided, so that she needn't be carried up and down the stairs to the bedroom. Besides, she could watch everyone and know what went on around the house all the time. The rest of us went upstairs. A little spare room was offered to Uncle Lee. Eventually this room would be rented to refugees from Russia to supplement our precarious family budget.

In the large sleeping room, there stood a big bed in the corner, the first one I had ever seen in our house. Of course, it was meant for Papa and Umma. The Korean bedding we had brought with us was rolled out on the floor beside the bed. There, my three brothers and I lay down. Umma was girlishly shy and fussed with the baby and pretended to be nursing her. A wooden partition separated the room from a little space adjacent to the stairway. In this space, another set of bedding was spread for Sister Alice and Sister Elizabeth. The lights were turned off. Then I complained of thirst and started for downstairs, telling Umma that I knew where there was a faucet.

"No! No! No!" Papa cried out, "you must never drink any water from the faucet." Then he further warned me, "You never drink cold water here in China." Umma came downstairs with me and poured a cup of hot tea from the teapot which was always kept warm in a padded potholder. My first lesson on life in China. As I lay beside my brothers with a warm cotton quilt over me, I wondered and waited for Umma to join Papa in bed. But suddenly I was overcome with sleep. Through all my childhood years, I never saw Umma in bed with Papa; she always waited for everyone to be asleep, and she was up and about long before anyone awoke in the morning.

8

THE
REVOLUTIONARY

EARLY IN FEBRUARY OF 1919 a secret meeting of Korean leaders took
place in Seoul. It was held in a little pharmacist's room in the Severance
Hospital located a scant mile away from the Great South Gate. Its mission was to draw up plans for the people's uprising against Japanese
colonial rule. My father was one of the eight leaders at that secret meeting. I learned of the founding session of the Korean revolution only
after my arrival in Shanghai a year later. This internationally governed
city of Shanghai had been chosen for the seat of the budding Korean
Independence Movement because the multinational controls of the city
provided a great measure of protection from the Japanese. I also discovered that my father, a fire-and-brimstone Christian minister, was now a
leading "Hyung-Myung-Ja," which literally meant "Life-Sacrificing-
Man"—a revolutionary.

    Was this my father? I beheld his face in wonderment. Yes, it was
the same broad, open handsome face: thick eyebrows shading his spar-
kling eyes, the prominent nose, the generous mouth. He stood there
tall and proud as always. In Korea, he had been a Christian minister
whose ringing voice shook the rafters of the immense Jung Dong First
Methodist Church and brought forth hundreds of men and women to
be baptized as Christians. The same man of dignity was now standing
there in Shanghai, a revolutionary, a "Life-Sacrificing-Man." But there
seemed hardly any difference; his role as a revolutionary was no less

dedicated than his work in the Christian ministry. This was the man who, when asked why he had chosen Christianity, answered, "Because I believed Jesus was more militant than Buddha."

The impetus for the historic Korean Independence Movement came from the declaration of the American president, Woodrow Wilson, before the Paris Peace Conference of World War I. There he had proclaimed "the right of all nations for self-determination." Inspired, the Koreans sent a secret emissary, Dr. Kim Kiu-Sik, to Paris to present Korea's demand for independence. President Wilson's response to Korea's cry for help was no different from that of another American president before him, Theodore Roosevelt. In 1905 when Japan first occupied Korea following her victory in the Russo-Japanese war, Korea turned to America for help, invoking the Mutual Aid Treaty of 1882 that existed between Korea and the United States. President Roosevelt not only reneged on U.S. obligations but insulted the Korean people by advising them to "cooperate with the Japanese." Now, a decade later, President Wilson too not only rejected Korea's plea but refused to allow any hearing of the Korean cause at the Peace Conference.

Despite such discouragement, the eight men in the pharmacist's room in Seoul charted the course of struggle for Korean independence and mapped out all the details for the uprising. The date: March first at sunrise. The locations: all major cities throughout the country. The method: nonviolent demonstration. The leaders banked on absolute secrecy for the success of their plan. To compose, print, and distribute the Declaration of Independence; to fabricate and deliver thousands of the forbidden Korean national flag; to appoint local leaders and transmit all instructions—to accomplish all this and more in secret, under the very nose of the dreaded Japanese police, there had to be absolute faith and trust of the people. And because my father, as the national superintendent of Methodist Sunday Schools, could travel throughout the country freely, he assumed the role of emissary-courier to maintain contact with all the local leadership.

Of the seven men who met with Father on that day, I still remember the names and faces of two: Kim Pil-Soo, an ascetic-looking Christian minister, and Park Hee-Do, a tall, strong man, another minister from the northern city of Pyongyang. It was not by accident that nearly half of the leaders were Christian ministers. One of the first acts of Japan's rule in Korea was to abolish all the people's organizations, social, cultural, and religious, not to mention political societies. The Christian churches, however, were allowed to remain open, perhaps in repayment of the American support of their conquest of Korea. Flushed with triumph, little did the conquerers anticipate that the Koreans would flock to the churches seeking solace and contact with their own people. Out of such an explosive Christian movement came new leaders, my father among the first, who through Christianity sought to keep alive the people's hope. They fervently believed in the words of Jesus: "Follow me and I shall make you free." In the history of American missionaries, no nation had converted overnight from their ancient religion to Christianity. Yet that is what happened in Korea following its conquest by Japan.

The timing of the revolt was ideal: the death of Korea's last king in the spring of 1919. He could not have chosen a more propitious moment to die. People from all corners of the country tracked their way to Seoul in a pilgrimage to attend the king's funeral. What better time to contact all the leaders of the country without arousing any suspicion? Another source of help to guarantee the success of the uprising was the Japanese police force itself. Their contempt for the Koreans was so comprehensive that they came to believe their own propaganda about "the lazy, stupid, good-for-nothing Koreans." Their arrogant mentality provided a perfect insulation against any possible detection or even suspicion of the plot. Anticipating a long struggle, the leaders established themselves as the "directors" of the Korean Independence Movement. Among the officers elected were Lee Syung-Hoon, chairman; Ham Tai-Young, secretary; and Soon Hyun, my father, chief of diplomacy. In accepting the high office, Father, with his typical humility, said, " I am a preacher. A preacher is the servant of all."

Late in the evening of February 22, 1919, another secret meeting was held in Seoul. It was an important caucus to select a foreign emissary. Charged with this responsibility were three directors of the newly formed Korean Independence Movement: Lee Syung-Hoon, the chairman; my father; and Chai Rin, personal representative of Sohn Pyun-Hee, the head of Chun-Do Kyo. Chun-Do Kyo, the Heavenly Way, was the only indigenous religion of Korea and was bearing the major financial burden of the movement. Actually, the caucus was being held to determine whether or not the job of representing the movement to the outside world could be entrusted to my father. Many personal and lengthy questions were directed at him not so much regarding his qualifications but to ascertain his readiness to sacrifice his life, if necessary, for the cause. Father's direct and honest answers—his usual response to all challenges—impressed the leaders of Father's convictions and determination. With their formal approval, a large sum of money was given to Father for travel and other anticipated expenses. Again, with his typical honesty, he kept only the amount he believed he needed and gave the rest, not to his family of eight children, but to his church. His family, he was assured, would be looked after by the treasurer, Park Hee-Do.

Three directives were given to Father: First, escape from the country immediately; second, proceed to the Manchurian city of Mukden; and third, contact other Korean patriots who would gather there. Escaping from Korea was not an easy matter. There was only one route: by train over the Yalu River from the Korean border town of Shin Eu-Ju to the Chinese city of Fung-Ten. Of course, the border crossing was patrolled by a horde of Japanese police and spies. I couldn't imagine Father shedding his Western clothes and disguising himself as a poor peasant carrying a pitiful-looking bundle. But he did. Even then, his escape through the cordon of spies was nothing short of a miracle. Once in China, again to evade the network of Japanese spies along the major routes of Manchuria, he traveled by devious routes and reached the city of Mukden.

In this teeming industrial city, Father's mission began in earnest. Among the Korean patriots Father was to contact in Mukden, the most important was a certain young man who was coming from Japan to meet him. The mysterious person, Father was told, was a fiery young fighter named Chai Chang-Sik. According to the instructions, Father was to meet this young man at a Chinese business establishment called the Hai-Chun Company. He found the business location and waited there, but no one appeared to meet him. He returned to the designated meeting place for several days, but always at different hours so as not arouse any suspicion. Father was frustrated, and growing increasingly anxious he even revealed his identity to the proprietor. Still there was no contact. His funds were dwindling and soon he would have to proceed to Shanghai where the center for the Korean Independence Movement was to be established. He made yet another secret visit to the Hai-Chun Company, then finally gave up.

He made his way to the Mukden railway station to begin the first leg of his journey to Shanghai. Moments before he was to board the train, a young man appeared and introduced himself; it was Chai Chang-Sik, the man Father had been looking for so desperately. Chai said that he knew of Father's visits to the Hai-Chun Company, but he had to be sure that he was really the Reverend Soon Hyun. He had followed Father to the railway station, and when he discovered that Father was proceeding to Shanghai, he finally felt sure of Father's identity. But they did not dare show their jubilation for fear of attracting attention and suspicion. Instead, they conferred hurriedly and agreed to travel separately and meet again in the city of Tientsin.

When they rejoined each other on the train at Tientsin for the long ride to Shanghai, they felt safe at last. Eagerly they exchanged news from Korea and Japan. Chai was jubilant to learn about the planned uprising. He regretted that the Korean émigrés living in Japan had not been allowed to participate, but understood the enormous risk involved in such a move. Once the movement was unleashed, Chai believed, the Koreans in Japan would rally, too, and support the movement.

My father and Chai arrived in Shanghai on the historic day of March First. Korea was aflame with cries of *"Man Sei! Man Sei! Man Sei!"* All the painstaking plans the eight leaders had mapped out in that tiny pharmacist's room in Seoul had been fulfilled. The absolute secrecy of the plan caught the Japanese police completely off guard. For two days they watched helplessly while millions of Koreans all over the country marched and shouted, *"Man Sei! Man Sei! Man Sei!"* But on the third day the police and soldiers attacked. That was the day when I walked to the palace grounds in Seoul and witnessed the slaughter of young students by the Japanese mounted marines.

Korean patriots and exiles gathered in Shanghai from around the world. Some of them Father had contacted in Manchuria and persuaded to join the movement in Shanghai. They were all in a state of excitement. Moving from one hotel to another to evade the Japanese spies,

Father met and consulted with all of them, conveying to them the instructions from the directors in Seoul. By some ingenious method, Chai Chang-Sik had smuggled a copy of the Declaration of Korean Independence. It needed to be translated into Chinese and English. Father worked with Lee Kwang-Soo on the English translation while Cho Dong-Ho worked on the Chinese. The headquarters of the Korean Independence Movement was established in the French Concession with Father as its secretary-general. It was safer there, for the Japanese could not conduct any search and seizure without official permission of the French authorities. The French were openly sympathetic to Korean revolutionaries and always forewarned them of any impending Japanese raid. On March 4, 1919, Father formally released the news of the Korean uprising. The news release, together with copies of the Declaration of Korean Independence, was given to the Chinese newspapers and the Associated Press. Thus it was my father who flashed the news of the Korean revolt around the world.

Pursuing this diplomatic mission, Father searched for aid from the outside world. First, he contacted the Americans. He met the Reverend George A. Fitch who became quite sympathetic and introduced Father to other influential Americans. These contacts later proved invaluable in providing shelter and protection for the Korean revolutionaries. Father also sought an audience with Sun Yat-sen, first president of the Republic of China. He had great hopes of receiving not only moral encouragement but also some material aid from this "Father of the Chinese Revolution." His hopes were completely shattered when he received Sun's curt message instructing Father to submit all requests to his aide. Even the Chinese president, like the American president before him, was afraid to help the Koreans for fear of ruffling the imperial feathers of Japan.

Father's search for help next took him to Peking accompanied by his good friend, Chai Chang-Sik. There he met and conferred with a group of Chinese revolutionaries who were charting their own struggle against the Japanese encroachment. Together, they explored vital areas of mutual interest and the possibilities of mutual aid and collaboration. Father also met an English journalist, L. B. Simpson, whom he persuaded to go into Korea and write an eyewitness report of the people's struggle. Simpson helped to organize a forum of international journalists where Father presented Korea's case and pleaded for all possible help. Both the general secretary and the Chinese secretary of the Peking YMCA were sympathetic and introduced Father to the secretary of the U.S. legation in Peking, Charles A. Terny. He, too, was supportive but regretted that his hands were tied with respect to any direct help. Nevertheless, he did help Father to meet other American officials as well as the general secretary of the Shanghai YMCA. These and many other new contacts established in Peking proved to be invaluable; they not only widened the circle of "Friends of Korea" but also opened a new source of funds so desperately needed by the movement.

Father and Chai returned to Shanghai near the end of March to find more patriots and exiles gathered there. They had all suffered hardship and had faced the danger of capture by the Japanese to reach Shanghai—from Japan, Siberia, Manchuria, and even from Seoul. Their overriding concern was to form a central governing body of the independence movement. While agreeing with the idea, but remembering the directives he had received in Seoul, Father counseled them not to make any final decision without the advice of the leadership in Seoul. The first step in the formation of a central body was the establishment of the Consultative Committee which would be charged with the task of founding a provisional parliament. The Korean patriots in exile elected the first such parliament, which was comprised of fourteen members that included my father. His major interest, however, remained in the field of diplomacy. Through the ever-changing underground channels, he was able to maintain contact with Korea and smuggle out news and photographs of the struggle and release them to the press. The most dramatic report was the Japanese massacre in Soowon, a little farming town near Seoul. A documented account together with pictures of the victims was obtained and given to the Chinese and the Western press. Through such work, Father was able to win many new "Friends of Korea," among them a Lieutenant Matinak of the U.S. Navy who later was to save Father and his colleagues from capture and certain death at the hands of the Japanese.

Another major undertaking of the movement at this time was the mounting of guerrilla warfare against the Japanese military forces moving into Manchuria. In the early 1920s, Japan was already laying the groundwork to take over the vast resources of Manchuria. Under the pretext of helping Chang Tso-lin, the Chinese warlord, to fight the bandits, Japan began to pour its troops into Manchuria. A handful of Korean guerrillas offered the only resistance, their daring raids inflicting considerable damage and interrupting Japan's timetable for the conquest. Eventually, however, Japan was to gain complete control and establish a puppet state by the name of Manchukuo.

Other young volunteers followed the clandestine route and conducted revolutionary activities inside Korea. In the midst of the fearful Japanese police, the young patriots organized and carried out every conceivable type of sabotage. There were even instances of open defiance in the form of strikes by workers and farmers. Under the leadership of the young fighters, the people carried out ingenious slowdowns in the factories and passive resistance in the countryside. Old people and young children often took part in these dangerous underground activities, inspiring everyone and keeping their spirit alive for the national struggle.

Now the revolutionary leaders in Shanghai were ready to form the Provisional Government of Independent Korea. Father's role in this vital step was to travel once again to far corners and bring other known leaders to Shanghai. Ahn Chang-Ho, known as a great orator and educator and living in the United States at the time, was contacted and persuaded to come and join the movement. Father sailed secretly to Hong Kong where he met Ahn and brought him safely to Shanghai. Next, he had to go to the Russian port city of Vladivostok and find Lee Dong-Hee, a former colonel in the old Korean army. To make certain of the mission's success, two aides accompanied Father. They had to travel across Manchuria which was practically under Japanese control. But they did penetrate this hostile territory and safely reached their destination. In Vladivostok, after much searching, Father found the Korean military leader and persuaded him to join the revolutionary group in Shanghai.

Father and his colleagues then faced a new problem: how to return to Shanghai safely. Using the same Manchurian route was out of the question, for the Japanese, fully alerted, were now on the lookout for them. Growing quite impatient, the Japanese authorities launched a daring move to capture my Father and his compatriots while they were still in Vladivostok. With more than a hundred soldiers, they laid a seemingly inescapable trap. That's when Father's new friend, the U.S. naval officer, came to his aid. Lieutenant Matinak not only spirited them out of the trap but also put them on board a Russian ship sailing to Shanghai. Once again, Father had successfully fulfilled his mission.

Upon their safe arrival in Shanghai, they were richly rewarded by being invited to the dedication ceremony of the Korean Provisional Government on November 1, 1919. The founding cabinet members were Syngman Rhee, premier; Ahn Chang-Ho, minister of the interior; Kim Kiu-Sik, minister of foreign affairs; Lee Dong-Hee, minister of military affairs; Lee See-Young, minister of legal affairs; Chai Chai-Myung, minister of finance; and Moon Chang-Bum, minister of communications. My father was elected vice-minister of foreign affairs and the first member of the Provisional Parliament. An imposing brick building in the French Concession was secured to house the newly formed government. Under the command of Kim Koo, a corps of twenty young revolutionaries was organized to provide security for the government. From such a humble beginning as the chief of guards, it was he, Kim Koo, who was to defy the whole world and keep the Provisional Government alive to its bitter end.

The birth of the Korean Provisional Government itself was a monumental achievement. It was accomplished in the midst of mounting difficulties both inside and outside Korea. The leaders had come from different areas with divergent views and backgrounds. It was inevitable, then, that there should rise conflicting interests and intense rivalry. And such a divisive factor was further compounded by the traditional mistrust between the northern and southern Koreans. The mutual mistrust, verging on hatred, grew out of deep roots. In the beginning of the fifteenth century when the Koryu dynasty was overthrown and the Yi dynasty established, for nearly five hundred years the people of the north were barred from all official positions and relegated to a subservient class. These "sins of the fathers" were now visited on their sons in Shanghai. Keeping the movement alive in the face of such factionalism demanded the utmost mental and physical resources. Moreover, most of the financial support came from the beleaguered people in Korea: trickles of money secretly collected and smuggled out to Shanghai. There was very little support from the outside world. No country offered any material aid—indeed, all were hesitant even to express moral support.

The newly born Soviet Union was fully occupied with its own struggle against the attacks of the Western powers who were determined to destroy it. Other European countries were equally occupied in emerging from the devastation of World War I and fighting for a place in the new alignment of the victor nations. Even China, Korea's natural ally, was too fearful of Japan's expansionist designs. China was afraid that any aid to the Korean rebellion might trigger Japan's attack.

The only ones who might have helped were the millions of dispossessed and oppressed peoples of Asia. But in 1919 they were not yet ready to raise their voices, not even for their own freedom. In the midst of such indifference and outright hostility, to have raised the voice of revolt, to have waved the national flag in the face of their conquerer, and to have waged a major struggle for independence with their Provisional Government in Shanghai—these were the deeds of a proud and brave people. These first cries in the Far East wilderness for national freedom had not been raised in vain, for they offered inspiration and hope and beat out a new path for the oppressed peoples of India, Indonesia, and Indochina and eventually even helped to awaken the "Sleeping Giant," China.

9

LIFE IN SHANGHAI

AT LAST, the tedious, miserable life on the road came to an end; no more the clatter of the train engulfing us day and night, no more wooden benches for beds and bowls of noodles for meals. We had to marvel how our little band of refugees, Uncle Lee and our tiny Umma with her eight young children, endured the long journey and reached our destination safely. And to have found our father who had prepared a home for us to live in! But before our rejoicing subsided, we became aware of some totally unexpected problems: how to adjust and adapt to the strange new surroundings. It seemed, in a matter of days, we had been torn from the land of our ancestors and tossed into another people's land. The Chinese, who were the subject of our jokes and jeers in Korea, were now at home and we were the intruders. How to deal with such a turnabout, how to fit into the new way of life, how to communicate with the sea of people, all speaking a strange language—these were the new, pressing problems facing us.

The challenge, however, did not faze us young ones. We children not only accepted but were delighted with everything new and strange. It aroused our curiosity to unravel anything appearing mysterious. We had an instinctive keenness for sounds of the Chinese language and could reproduce them without much difficulty. We thoroughly enjoyed mimicking the Chinese children, and soon we began to understand and speak Chinese.

I began to venture out into the city alone in ever widening circles, exploring and testing my newly acquired language, finding directions, bargaining with street vendors to buy water chestnuts and sweet dumplings on sticks for snacks. Sometimes, I would ride the streetcar far off to the Whangpoo River to sit by the muddy water's edge and watch the bobbing sampans, the plodding, stately junks, and the menacing foreign battleships. I began to feel quite comfortable with my adopted country. But then I watched my younger brothers. They seemed much more at home than I, chattering away with the neighborhood children in Chinese. David, my youngest brother, surprised even the elderly Chinese by arguing and quarreling with the children in Chinese, and holding his own.

It wasn't quite so easy for my two big sisters, Elizabeth and Alice. They were forced to remain indoors most of the time as was customary for young ladies in China. Umma wouldn't even allow them to go with her to the marketplace. Their only contact with the outside world was on some special occasion when the whole family would go to a Korean community gathering or, even more rarely, on a family outing. They occupied themselves doing the family chores: cooking, sewing, cleaning, and washing. As dreary as their lives must have been, I never heard them grumbling.

But what about their education? My father and mother would not dream of allowing them to become like the women of the old world— to spend their lives doing housework and bearing children. So, somehow, they found a way and had my sisters enrolled in a women's boarding school in Shanghai. By living and attending classes together with the Chinese young ladies, they could learn the language and continue their high school education. They were also given a taste of the arts such as music and drama. One evening, the family went to see a performance in sisters' school. I was thrilled to see Sister Alice appear on stage taking part in the play. She was so beautiful and she spoke in Chinese so clearly, my whole being swelled with pride. On weekends, they were allowed to leave school and come home to visit. What stories they had to tell us! In rapt attention, we would listen to their recounting of all the strange and funny incidents, of the endless rules of deportment, and of the daily unpleasant encounters with students and teachers arising out of misunderstandings. It seemed their living and studying in the Chinese women's boarding school was terribly trying. Still, they persevered and survived through the end of the school year.

LIFE IN SHANGHAI

My invalid sister Soon-Ok became bedridden shortly after our arrival in Shanghai. A pretty canopied bed was placed in a corner of the living room downstairs where she spent all her days and nights. Propped up in bed, she could survey all the goings-on in the house and participate in the intrigues of her brothers and sisters. When Father brought his colleagues home for dinner and talk, Sister Soon-Ok would eagerly listen to their conversation and thus keep abreast of the Korean independence movement. When I came home from school, I would always leave my bundle of books at her bedside so that she could use them and carry on her own studies. Sometimes she would question me on some subject, but more often it was I who asked for her help with my homework. In fact, she should be credited largely for my passing grades in mathematics, history, and geography. So anxious was she to learn, at every opportunity, she would even study her big sisters' books. In spite of her cheerful spirit, her physical condition visibly worsened; the enforced immobility brought on problems which wracked her with constant pain. Only her intense interest in learning and her emotional involvement with the people around her helped to ease the pain and even share some of the fun with us.

If life's heavy burdens ever discouraged Umma, she never showed it. She planned and she toiled, and against all odds she was determined to preserve a bit of Korea in the wilderness of the foreign city. So at least once a day, she would feed us Korean food, and at every opportunity, she would remind us and teach us Korean manners and traditions. But her teachings were always amusing and delightful, for she would teach us by telling a pungent Korean proverb, a wise saying of a sage, or a very funny folktale. She refused to learn to speak Chinese. Instead, she spoke to all the Chinese people in Korean as though she was still in Seoul. She did condescend, however, to learn to count in Chinese and picked up a few other words she needed in her daily dealings with the merchants. Even with such a limited vocabulary, she was quite proficient in bargaining with the tradesmen. And all the merchants respected her not for her eloquence but for her commanding manners and the cutting tone of her voice. Her favorite Chinese words were: "No good!" "Too much!" and "You cheat!"

The "house" we lived in presented some inconveniences. The sleeping arrangements remained the same as the first night of our arrival, but we, the eight children, were growing so rapidly that the space allocated to each kept shrinking. It was not really a house but one of four apartments built into a long narrow building. Rows of these buildings were divided into two sections with a central corridor which led to the street. The entire development was walled-in and was called a "compound." These compounds, some small and simple and others large and elaborate, spread over the city and housed most of the working people.

But the poorer people, I discovered later, lived away from the International Settlement in outlying areas called the "Chinese Section." Here, the little old-fashioned Chinese houses were built of crude mud-bricks, and when I first walked through the narrow, unpaved streets, I was overcome with the oppressive congestion. In some areas there were no houses to speak of but only indescribable squalor. The open sewers, the outdoor cooking over wooden stoves everywhere, and the ever-present milling masses of people saturated the entire Chinese Section with a peculiar odor. In stark contrast, our apartment in the French Concession, one of a hundred units in a compound with running water, would have to be considered luxurious. It was quite spacious and fairly comfortable. There was only one serious problem; there was no toilet.

The facility provided for that purpose was a wooden barrel with an ill-fitting cover, hidden away in a dark corner. In our home, it was placed in a tight space under the stairway. But the receptacle always made its presence known, especially toward the end of the day and in the summertime. Fortunately, we had an "Am-Ma," a maid, whose first duty upon arriving for work each morning was to carry the offensive barrel out of the house and leave it at the front door. Of course, the hundred families living in the compound all did the same. Eventually, a pony-drawn cart with a wooden tank would roll through the alleys, and the driver would dump the contents of all the barrels into the tank. The barrels then would be washed and scrubbed and taken back into the homes for another day's service. During the morning hour of the barrel ritual, the air would be laden with the stench throughout the city. This was in 1920—and Shanghai was the most modern city in all China!

Another drastic change had to do with what we wore. To avoid being conspicuous and pointed at, we shed our Korean clothes and dressed ourselves like all the others. Sisters Alice and Elizabeth wore the fashionable clothes of Chinese young ladies: tight-fitting silk blouses with high collars and short pleated skirts. I thought they were very becoming. In time, even Umma succumbed and wore the Chinese costume, but in subdued somber colors and with a pair of long pants instead of the short skirt. As for Sister Soon-Ok and baby Sister Mary, since they didn't have to face the outside world, Umma dressed them in odd-looking Western dresses she bought in a store.

Finally, Umma took us boys to the Wing-On Company, the biggest store I had ever seen. Inside the multistory building, there were many different kinds of little stores on every floor. I learned that it was called a "Department Store." Umma led us to the clothing store and fitted us with Western clothes for boys: white shirt with short sleeves, tight pants with legs cut off above the knees, and a matching jacket with pockets and three large buttons in the front. A little cap perched on the head completed the very strange outfit. I didn't know whether to feel ashamed or proud of my new appearance. But soon I became accustomed and comfortable. I also began to like the sight of Umma and my sisters in their Chinese costume; they looked adorable.

In the midst of all the upheaval, one aspect of our family life remained constant; our evening dinner was always Korean. No one knew how or where Umma found all the necessary ingredients for the dishes. The many guests and visitors at our home always marveled at the variety of Korean food Umma served: the indispensable *kim-chee,* of course, *gak-doo-gi* (preserved radish), and *got-cho-jang* (hot chili paste). For Umma, these were only the basics. Soon she began to concoct more elaborate and fancy delicacies: honeyed chestnuts, preserved persimmon, *yak-bap* ("medicine rice"), nectar of pine nuts, and many others. Our home soon became a Korean social center just as it had always been in Korea, except that the visitors in Shanghai were not church workers; they were revolutionaries. They would drop in at all hours of the day and night. The older ones could always count on a delicious Korean meal, but the younger ones, I suspected, were more interested in staring at Sisters Alice and Elizabeth. They often brought presents of all kinds, especially for us children. Umma welcomed them all and took great delight in serving and watching them enjoying her food. They would reward her in turn with the latest news of the independence movement. Growing up in such a hospitable and convivial atmosphere, we all learned early in our childhood to enjoy people and their company.

Umma never got used to the daily trip to the marketplace. On the days I didn't go to school, she would always take me with her. It was a huge market occupying half of a street block, partly roofed but mostly in the open. It was always crowded from early dawn until late afternoon. Umma would always go in the early hours so the supplies would be plentiful and fresh. As we approached, I could breathe the smells in the air and hear the muffled drone of the people. A common sight along the market was that of the people with bundles of clothes and towels under their arms hurrying along to the public bathhouse. There were countless numbers of stands and stalls loaded with vegetables and fruits, fish and meats, and a myriad of household utensils, baby clothes, cotton shoes and slippers, and many strange objects whose purpose and use I couldn't even guess. The merchants vied with each other shouting out their goods, the shoppers outshouting the tradesmen to bargain, the children screaming either with pleasure or pain. Together they raised a deafening din.

But arising above the noise of the crowd were the pitiful cries of the beggars. I learned that they were no ordinary beggars; they were "graduates" of the "Beggars College" on the outskirts of the city. Indeed, they had completed a rigorous course of study in the technique of wringing people's hearts and prying open their purses. There were beggars holding up an arm with the hand chopped off and beggars dragging a leg with its foot missing, fresh blood dripping and congealing. These were some of the masterpieces created at the "Beggars College." The people knew that all the gory wounds were artificial, but they looked so real, they cringed at the sight, tossed a few coins, and hurried away.

The most gruesome sight I ever saw was a man whose bare chest was pierced by a long steel pin; this was no makeup, it was real. Over the pin was hung a heavy iron chain at the end of which a huge iron ball was tied. By walking backwards slowly, the beggar dragged the heavy burden by the pin stuck in his chest, his animal-like scream accompanying each step. Only when he stooped to retrieve the coins thrown at him did the tearing of his chest momentarily stop. This man-made horror was beyond all imagination, and the sheer, shocking sight of it brought out a few more coins than others.

Some days at the market, I would stroll past the row of shops that were alive with sights, sounds, and smells. One of the most fascinating was the apothecary's shop. The shelves were lined with bottles and jars of all shapes and sizes containing strange herbs, dried insects, snakes, and mysterious skins and bones. The only incentive for lingering on at this store was the pleasant scent of burning incense. I also liked to look at the bright silk shop, rolls of fabrics stacked high up to the ceiling and splashes of silk with intricate designs brilliant colors hanging on the wall as in a palace chamber. The music of a lone flute floated from the shop enticing the passersby to enter.

My favorite, of course, was the sweetshop. It had so many varieties of candies, cookies, and pastries, I never could have tasted them all. At each visit, I would spend my precious coins and select a new item for yet another delicious experience.

Winter in Shanghai could be quite dreary. It was never really cold and it never snowed. But the sky was always gray, the trees bare, and the air very damp. All outdoor activities diminished. There were fewer people riding the streetcars, and even at the marketplace there were fewer crowds, less shouting. The subdued winter of the city, however, did not keep me and my friends from enjoying ourselves. We had only to change the games from baseball and basketball to soccer and rollerskating. Just the same, the winter was always too long, and we waited impatiently for the approach of spring. Even before there was any visible green on the branches of the willows and the poplars, I would begin to whisper in Umma's ear about a springtime family picnic. It was my way of arousing Umma's own nostalgic memories. Every day now, all of us children would exclaim how warm the weather was and how much fun we had at our last picnic in Korea. Finally, we overheard Father and Umma whispering to each other, and we knew that there would be a family picnic soon.

It was such a long wait for the spring! Finally, Father announced the date of our picnic. The day before the great event, Umma and my big sister worked all day preparing food. I could hardly sleep that night and got up early in the morning. I looked outside; the day was bright and warm and beautiful, a perfect day for our first outing in China. Father's good friend Chai Chang-Sik and his pretty secretary, Kim Ai-Young, came to join us. The pretty secretary was an especially bright young woman with a college education who had escaped from Korea and stolen her way to Shanghai. Soon other guests arrived: the exuberant young revolutionaries. The young men were all admirers of my father and, not so secretly, of my two big sisters.

With everything ready, we walked to catch the streetcar which would take us to the outskirts of the city. The young people gladly carried all the boxes, bundles, and baskets, and took turns carrying Sister Soon-Ok on their backs. It was a happy walk, and the young men vied with each other to be funny and entertaining. Mainly for the benefit of Umma and my big sisters, they pranced, joked, and laughed. They also teased and shot friendly barbs at the somber and serious young man who refused to be drawn into their buffoonery. He smiled at their jokes, but when their teasing grew somewhat reckless, he stopped it with a sharp command. I learned to like this serious young man. He was very gentle and kind, but also determined and dedicated to becoming the leader of the young revolutionaries. In later years, he smuggled himself into Korea and led the underground independence movement throughout World War II. He was my idol. He became the hero of all the Korean people, too, and the number one enemy of the Japanese police. His name was Park Huen-Young.

We got off the streetcar and walked along the country road. But unlike Korea, there were no mountains or streams, no clusters of azalea and dogwood blossoms. Only flat farmland stretched ahead of us, and on the farms we saw men, women, and children working with bent backs. They plodded slowly, some of them carrying enormous bundles on their heads while others carried even heavier loads suspended on the ends of a pole. Suddenly someone yelled, "Look! Look over there!" On the distant horizon we could see bursting clouds of bright pink in the middle of which rose the outline of a beautiful pagoda; the whole view was a classical brush painting in space. It was the peach orchard, our chosen picnic ground. Bubbling with new excitement, we hurried our steps, the children breaking into a run.

As we walked under the clouds of peach blossoms, everyone took deep breaths of the delicious, perfumed air. "Oh, this is the spot for our picnic!'' Father announced at a clearing. Umma spread a large sheet on the ground and the young men put down all the boxes, baskets, and bundles. Straw mats were rolled out where Sister Soon-Ok was set down, and others joined her, stretching their legs and groaning with relief from the long walk. Then everyone began talking at once; some praised the beautiful orchard while others recalled other orchards they had seen in Korea. In the midst of the commotion and excitement, with the help of Sisters Elizabeth and Alice, Umma calmly went about opening the boxes and baskets and spreading out the picnic feast.

Father waved his arms and asked for quiet. "While walking along the farms," he said, "I composed a poem. Please listen and see what you think." He cleared his throat, and fixing his eyes in distant space, he began to chant his poem. It was in Chinese in the classic form. Everyone, especially Father's colleagues, listened raptly. I couldn't understand the Chinese words but I enjoyed listening to Father's melodious, ringing voice. When he finished his chanting, he interpreted the poem in Korean. In the classical style of poetry, the consummate idea was always expressed in the final line. In Father's poem, the last line was an eloquent description of the Korean people's longing for their homeland. The listeners burst into applause. Teacher Chai was next to compose and recite his poem followed by a few other elders. All ended their compositions with feelings of nostalgia: some for missing family and friends, some for the pine-filled mountains and winding rivers, and one for the sight of pretty young ladies in flowing skirts and tight-fitting blouses.

"Jot-ta! Jot-ta!"

"Bravo! Bravo!"

Each poem was greeted with enthusiastic applause. Caught up in the mood, a young man broke out with the Korean people's favorite folk song: *"Arirang! Arirang! Arariyo!"* And everyone including women and children joined in singing the chorus. At the end of the chorus, someone would sing an improvised verse which would be followed by yet a louder chorus:

Arirang! Arirang! Arariyo!
Arirang Gogai-rul Numer-ganda!

CHAPTER 9

Arirang! Arirang! Arirang Mountain!
Over the Arirang Peak he must go!

This simple folk song grew out of Korean history. It tells the story of two lovers who were forced to separate. The man leaves his love and travels over Arirang Mountain. The lady laments and wishes him to suffer blistered feet and return to her. Different regions of the country developed different versions and styles of singing. But in contemporary times, the song began to bear political overtones. "Arirang Peak" became a symbol of death for political prisoners. To go over "Arirang Peak" meant a man's last journey to his execution.

A wave of nostalgia swept over the gathering; a long moment of silence. Then a lone voice broke the spell with a happy song:

Pak-Yun Pok-Po
Hurogo Narinan Mool-eun . . .

It was the song of Pak-Yun Waterfall, a famous scenic sight in the city of Kaesong. (The so-called Truce City of Panmunjon is located near this ancient capital of the Koryu kingdom.) This song painting the dramatic beauty of the waterfall was passed from generation to generation for over five hundred years. Others picked up the happier mood and sang one song after another; among others, the fun-loving "Playboy Song" and the ever popular song of "Doragi Digging"—a national pastime of Koreans in the spring. It is a common sight to see men, women, and children on the hillsides searching for *doragi* roots and digging them up. These white springtime roots, when boiled and marinated, make a most delicious salad with a unique, pleasant flavor. Now carried away by the jubilance, Father volunteered to sing his favorite song: "Bang-Ah Taryung," the "Rice-Pounding Song." When the rice is harvested in the fall, the farmer sings this song as he pounds the rice in a stone bin:

Eh! Heh! Ehehe Ya!
Eruha Gung-Gul Lurah!
Come on! Come on! Come on!
Let us roll and pound it!

Irung-sung! Jurung-sung! Hut-turujin Gun-sim!
Eryha Gung-Gul Lurah!
Sorrow here! Sorrow there! All empty sorrows!
Roll, roll! And pound all the sorrows away!

"With so much singing, you must all be starving." It was Umma's way of announcing the food was ready. Everyone stopped singing and fluttered around the feast set out on a white cloth. The sight alone was enough for all of us to exclaim: *"Aigo-cham! Aigo-cham!"* "Oh, really! Oh, really!"

Each one picked up a large bowl and filled it with rice and all kinds of delicacies, and Umma filled up smaller bowls for the little ones. As we began to eat, the only sounds heard were the clicking of chopsticks and appreciative cries of *"Aigo! Aigo-cham!"* "Really! But really!" This memorable day also marked the first time I tasted real American food. Some young man brought the strange food from the American store. He taught me their names: bread, butter, jam. Eating the heavenly slice of bread covered with butter and jam made me understand why the Americans kept their skin so white, their eyes so blue, and their noses so big.

When the great feast came to an end with many more cries of *"Aigo! Aigo-cham!"* the elders had another round of composing and reciting poems. I enticed my younger brothers, Paul and Joshua, to go with me to explore the pagoda. At close view, I was surprised and disappointed to find the beautiful pagoda so old and decrepit. The paint on the wall and the woodwork had long since faded and peeled off. It was rather sad to see some crumbling holes in the wall. Despite their fears, I persuaded my brothers to enter the pagoda. I led the way up the winding stairs. As we climbed, the stairway grew narrower and the steps creaked louder. We stopped on the fifth or the sixth story, and there, through an opening, we saw a sweeping, panoramic view. Below us we could see the entire exuberant peach orchard, the surrounding farms, and, in the distance, the majestic outline of the city of Shanghai. There were two or three more stories of the pagoda, but the growing creaks of the steps discouraged us from going any further. I took the hands of my brothers, rushed down the stairs, and ran out of the old pagoda.

Chapter 9

When we rejoined our party, they were already packing the boxes and baskets and rolling up the mats. I felt sad to see such a wonderful day come to an end. But the holiday spirit had already faded and people were discussing the shortest way home. The young men picked up all the bundles; one lifted Sister Soon-Ok, and another picked up little Brother David, and placed them on their shoulders. As we marched out of the orchard, heading for the streetcar, the young people accompanied their walk with their favorite students' marching song. The lively rhythm lightened the burden and revived everyone's spirits. I walked along with Umma and Sisters Alice and Elizabeth. Only one young man lagged behind and walked with us; it was Park Huen-Young, the silent one.

The next day after the picnic, it was hard for me to return to routine daily life. How much harder it must have been for Father, Teacher Chai, his pretty secretary, and all the young men to return to their thankless tasks. But Father and his colleagues had to return to search for new friends and money to support the Provisional Government, and for the young revolutionaries to find money and arms for the Korean guerrillas fighting the Japanese in Manchuria. And I had to return to my own routine: school everyday, baseball after school, and trips to the marketplace with Umma on Saturdays. Nonetheless, I refused to sink into a rut, and whenever I felt the need, I managed to find some form of diversion—a visit with a friend living in a distant neighborhood, a trip to the university to watch a soccer match, or a streetcar ride to the Bund to eat a cup of American ice cream and watch the parade of ships in the harbor. On Sunday afternoons, I would join a group of friends and go to the Shanghai racecourse. There, we watched the white people dashing about back and forth on horseback, driving a wooden ball with long-handled wooden mallets; they said the game was called "polo." All we could think of was how rich one must be to be playing "polo." We also watched the Englishmen play a game called "cricket." It seemed rather boring; I much preferred to watch the game of baseball played by Americans, mostly sailors from the American warships.

On one warm summer evening, the elders invited me to join them on an evening outing. I was surprised and delighted—all the more so when I discovered that their destination was Shin Sei Gai, "the New

World," a famous amusement park. I had heard many wondrous tales about this magic world but never expected to see it for myself. Because this was an evening excursion, only my two big sisters and I could go; Umma had to stay home with Sister Soon-Ok and the little ones. It was twilight when we arrived at the park. The multicolored lights and lanterns strung over the paths of the entire park were already lit. And when the evening darkness enveloped the park, they seemed to come alive and sparkled brilliantly. We strolled past the rows of stalls and stands where the hawkers contorted their faces and cried out to attract customers. The crowds of people were mesmerized by the sights of so many strange things brought from around the world to sell. In another part, there were painted tents where all kinds of exhibits and shows were in progress. What fascinated me in particular were the bright posters displayed in front of every stall: pictures of acrobats, dancers, puppeteers, magicians, sword swallowers, flame eaters, and many other unbelievable pictures. At my begging, Father took us to see the magic show. I was hypnotized by the magician; he was not a human but some being from another world with magic powers to make things disappear and reappear.

The high point of the magical evening was the Chinese opera theatre. The elders were excited and impatient as they waited in line to purchase tickets, the real reason for their coming to the park. Inside the theatre, I found another strange world where the people too behaved strangely. As soon as we sat in our seats, a vendor brought us a trayful of steaming hot towels. I watched the elders. They shook the towels and dabbed their faces and wiped their hands with them. When they finished, they dropped the towels on the little ledge attached to the backs of the seats in front. It seemed an odd ritual, but I imitated them as though I had done it all my life. To my surprise, I discovered that wiping one's face and hands with a hot towel could be a most exhilarating way to prepare oneself for the opera.

The vendor returned and picked up all the used towels. He then put down two large teapots and a stack of teacups on the ledge. Next, he picked out several little packages from his tray and placed them next to the teapots. I was fascinated and eagerly watched the elders to see what they would do. They poured the tea and passed the teacups to everyone. Then they opened the packages, picked out the contents, and began to crack them with their teeth. They would then sip the hot tea and wash down whatever they were chewing. I leaned over and picked out some of the contents of the packages. I was amazed! They were common ordinary seeds, pumpkin, watermelon, and sunflower seeds! Except these were salted and roasted. Cracking seeds and sipping hot tea—what a prelude to an opera! And this ceremony was going on throughout the whole theatre!

The cracking of seeds subsided somewhat when the musicians appeared on stage, each carrying an instrument and a portable stool. They proceeded to one side of the stage, sat on their stools, and began adjusting and tuning their instruments. There were many types of string and wind instruments and a variety of drums and cymbals. Then, without any conductor or announcement, they began to play. It was a blast of chaotic sounds; only the shrill melody of the string instruments kept it from total distortion. I listened intently and tried to discern the musical pattern. It was impossible; the discords, the unpredictable rhythm, and the disturbing cacophony completely frustrated me.

The music stopped just as abruptly as it had started. Silence. Loud pounding of the drum broke the silence; it began slowly and gradually accelerated in tempo and intensity. With the final flurry of the drums, the hero of the drama appeared. His elaborate and colorful costume and his imposing posture left little doubt that our hero was indeed a brave warrior. The shafts of flags he carried on his back, the multiplumed headdress, and the fierce masklike makeup on his face all attested to his noble station and character. Accompanied by deep drumbeats, he strutted downstage in slow, deliberate strides as befitting a proud hero. When the orchestra burst into a new discordant blast, our hero began to sing. He was recounting his personal history in battles and assuring the audience of his prowess as a warrior. His words, which the elders translated for me, were convincing and accompanied with graceful, sweeping gestures. Concluding his singing with a dramatic aria, he displayed his superb swordsmanship by flashing, slashing, lunging, and twirling his enormous ancient sword. His singing ended, he strutted over to one side and struck a majestic pose. The audience burst into applause and loud shouts of *"Hao! Hao! Ding Hao!* Bravo! Bravo! Bravo!"

Once again, the deep drumbeats brought another character on stage. He too wore an impressive costume: flags fluttering on his back and a fierce-looking mask painted on his face, all signifying that he too was a warrior. But the colors of his costume and even his makeup were distinctly different from those of the hero; they were all dark and somber. And instead of a sword, this warrior carried a long three-pronged spear. He began to sing of his valor and the many battles he had fought. He accompanied his singing with eloquent and threatening gestures. His unbelievable artistry with the spear, his lightning leaps and whirls in perfect rhythm with his singing, brought the audience to another roar: *"Hao! Hao! Ding Hao!"* Finishing his long aria, he swaggered to one side facing our hero and struck a menacing pose.

Now the deep drumbeats brought on stage a band of soldiers twirling their swords. The music became animated and lively as the soldiers took their station behind our hero. Another band of soldiers in dark uniform appeared on stage, performed their acrobatics, and took their station in back of the dark warrior. It appeared that a royal battle was about to erupt.

A long moment of silence and then, at last, an entrancing melody coming from a lone flute floated across the audience. The lights dimmed to semidarkness and a willowy, white figure appeared on stage: the heroine. She moved ever so gracefully toward the audience. I could discern her lovely glowing gown trimmed with silver and gold and the tiny crown with bright tassels perched on her head. In her delicate hand she carried a silk fan. Her simply made-up face was captivating: thinly painted black eyebrows, flushing, rosy cheeks, and burning red lips. Her beauty was almost unearthly. She began to sing in a high falsetto voice, and for the first time the orchestra accompanied her in muted tones. With delicate subtle gestures, she was singing the story of her long journey.

"Do you understand?" asked an elder sitting next to me.

"No," I answered in a whisper.

"Watch," he said. "She is mounting a horse to cross the mountain." Indeed, by her movements and pantomime I could visualize the horse and her graceful mounting followed by a difficult and arduous ride across the mountain.

"Now watch her carefully," the elder said. "She has descended from the mountain and has reached a riverbank. See her dismounting from the horse?" I couldn't believe how real all the drama on stage was, and the heroine was accompanying every scene with the most complicated and syncopated melody.

"Now, tell me," the elder said, "what do you think the lady is doing?"

"She is stepping onto something," I said.

"Yes," the elder agreed. "She is boarding a boat."

"What is she doing now?" I asked impatiently.

"She is sailing on the river. Look how the rough waves are rocking her boat."

The boat finally reaches the shore and the heroine alights. She turns to one side and, for the first time, notices our hero in his majestic pose. Happy in her discovery, she tiptoes across the stage close to him and renders a rapturous aria. Only then does she see the dark warrior at the opposite side, shaking with anger. She glides over to him and teases him with her fan, flicking it at his flags, his costume, and finally at his face. Unable to contain himself, the dark warrior leaps to the center stage and demonstrates his artistry with his spear. In response, our hero forces his adversary away and weaves a complex pattern of swordsmanship in the air. It is obvious both warriors are prepared to lay down their lives for the hand of the beautiful heroine.

A deafening outburst of drums and cymbals heralds the inevitable battle. The soldiers of the opposing warriors rush onto the center stage and engage in mass combat. The flashing of the swords, the leaping and tumbling to attack and retreat, the whirling mass of soldiers and swords bring the audience to the edge of their seats. At a command from the warriors, the soldiers halt their struggle and disappear, leaving the stage to their master warriors.

Now the mortal combat begins: the sword against the spear. The two rivals advance and face each other. Alternately, they sing their challenge and proclaim their vow to eliminate all who oppose them. The mood of their singing grows more ominous as they circle each other with weapons extended for an advantageous position. They charge and they clash, they spin and they whirl, they parry and retreat. The drumbeats and the clash of cymbals accelerate as the combat grows more fierce and more reckless. In the middle of a daring maneuver by the dark warrior, our hero cuts loose in a lightning attack, forcing his adversary to drop his spear and fall to the ground. The victor leaps and plants his heavy boot on the prostrate body and renders his victorious aria. The heavenly lady tiptoes to the conquerer and rewards him with an amorous melody while extending her silk fan to lightly brush the hero's cheek.

"Hao! Hao! Ding Hao! Ding Hao!" The whole audience came to life shouting their approval without restraint.

Coming out of the theatre, I couldn't stop talking about the beautiful heroine. "But don't fall in love with her," an elder cautioned me, and everyone burst into laughter. I was baffled and a bit angry about their laughing at me.

"Why? Why not?" I refuted them angrily. "And what are you all laughing about?"

"Well," the same elder said soothingly, "because the beautiful heroine is really a man." He then explained patiently, "In the Chinese opera, the heroine is always played by a man. The beautiful heroine you saw was played by a very famous actor named Mei Lan Fang." My disillusionment shattered me. But whenever I had the opportunity, I returned again and again to see Mei Lan Fang, who was to become a legend in the annals of Chinese opera.

Another treasured experience in Shanghai was my discovery of the American motion picture. We arrived there after a long streetcar ride and were greeted by blinding electric lights and huge posters of the actors hung along the wall. My friends led me up the stairs to the balcony. As soon as we took our seats, we were greeted by a vendor, not with hot towels and roasted seeds, but with chewing gum and candies. There was also music, not the cacophony of a Chinese orchestra, but the pleasant, rumbling music of a pipe organ. This American movie theatre was as strange as the Chinese opera theatre. The lights blinked out and the moving picture flashed on the enormous white screen. The organ continued to play throughout the whole show, sometimes soft and slowly, sometimes loud and swiftly, depending on what was happening on the screen.

The first movie I saw was called *Way Down East.* An actress named Lillian Gish played the part of the heroine. She was so fragile and beautiful, and the plot so sad, that I couldn't keep from crying. I could hardly contain myself when she was being carried away on an ice floe to be dashed over the waterfall. The audience began stamping and screaming.

"Stop! Stop! Stop!"

"Save her! Save her! Somebody, save her!"

I joined the people and yelled as loudly as I could. The theatre was in pandemonium. As though in response to our cries, at the last moment the heroine was snatched away and saved from the awful fate. I could hear the deep sigh of relief followed by a burst of applause.

Such a thrilling introduction to the American movie made me an addict for life. I saved every penny I could and went to the magic theatre again and again on Saturday afternoons. And I became quite familiar with the songs the organist played. But since I didn't know the words, I just hummed and whistled when I heard the organ play. Only years later did I discover the names of some of the tunes I was whistling: "My Old Kentucky Home," "Way Down Upon the Swanee River," "Old Black Joe," "Yankee Doodle," and "Stars and Stripes Forever"!

I also discovered Pola Negri—to me the most perfect actress of all. Quite different from Lillian Gish, she was not tiny and fragile. Nor was she weak and helpless; she was strong and commanding. Her movements were majestic and she walked so regally, whenever she appeared, that people stepped away to make room for her. In remembrance of such beauty, dignity, and pride, my firstborn daughter was named Paula—I didn't know that Negri's first name was not spelled that way!

When I had no money but lots of time, I would often go to the French Park. Located in the heart of the French Concession, it was famous for its immaculately manicured lawn and its exotic flower garden. Prominent signs were erected at every entrance to guard and protect the park. The signs read: "Dogs and Chinese Not Allowed." This was the kind of insult Europeans heaped on the Chinese people after having plundered their country for a century. Shanghai, China's largest and most modern port city, was one of the prizes of the West's "Battleship Diplomacy." It was a common sight to see a Chinese being beaten on the street by a Westerner with a cane. I often saw Western sailors spitting on and kicking the rickshaw pullers who had carted them around the city all day and were begging to be paid. "Dogs and Chinese Not Allowed"—the sign was the embodiment of all the humiliation and insults the Chinese people were forced to endure.

I was allowed to enter the French Park because I wore Western clothes. But why did I go there, and keep going back? I was incurably curious and not a little jealous. I had to find out what the forbidden world was like and see what the privileged people did in their guarded sanctuary. At first sight, I was astounded by the painstaking care of the lawn and the flower garden; they seemed better cared for than our home. Even the white swans gliding around the pond appeared insolent and proud. Then I saw the Western men and women behaving like other people. For the first time in Shanghai, I saw them frolicking and laughing. Dressed in brief, flimsy clothes, they were running and yelling while chasing a little white ball. They were really playing—playing tennis, the same game I saw the Americans play in Seoul.

Life in Shanghai was not always adventure and fun. In fact, most of the time it was a dreary struggle. There were times when the whole family would sink into a deep depression, most often because of the lack of money. But the most depressing moment for me was when Father and Umma quarreled. The argument would begin in hushed voices to keep it from the children's ears. But as their frustration mounted, their voices would rise to the point of shouting at each other. It pained me to hear Umma scolding Father for being too gentle and reticent.

"Why are you always the last one to receive money?" Umma would chide him. "Why don't you let them know your children are starving and insist on getting your share of the money first?"

Father would be speechless and the explode, "I am not a beggar!"

Such distressing moments usually ended with Umma leaving the house, most of the time taking me with her. She would go straight to the home of the treasurer and refuse to leave until she got the money to meet the crisis. The treasurer was a gentle person who would try to explain that there was no money in the treasury.

"Then you'd better go and find some, because I'm not leaving until I get some money." The treasurer knew that it was not an empty threat, and somehow he would scrape up the money for Umma. Once again the family crisis was over. After supper, Father would make us all laugh by imitating Umma screaming.

The financial resources of the Provisional Government continued to shrink so that not even the top officials could be sustained. We were forced to move to a cheaper place in the Chinese tenement district. Even then, we didn't always have food on the table. Umma's visits to the market became more rare, and eventually she even gave up going to the treasurer's home. Now we had only one meal a day, and waiting for food the little ones would cry with hunger. Unable to prolong the wait, Umma would hand me a few pennies and a bowl and dispatch me to the noodle shop. When I returned, Umma would carefully dish out the noodles in little bowls so that everyone would have some. The soup was watery and there were not enough noodles, but it was hot and it helped to stave off our hunger. This painful period lasted quite a while until one day someone brought us some money, our family's share of the precious money smuggled out of Korea.

Our new house was on the fringe of a neighborhood where the street vendors and rickshaw pullers lived. These people lived in abject poverty, but when they discovered we were Koreans, they looked down on us and began calling us names. We pretended to ignore them, but we could hardly bear it when we heard them jeer: *"Wang Guo Loo! Wang Guo Loo!"* True, we were the people of a conquered nation, but to be called "Slave of a Lost Country" by these poverty-stricken and ignorant laborers was more than we could bear. It reached a breaking point on a hot summer afternoon when a group of Chinese boys came to our front door and began taunting us: *"Wang Guo Loo! Wang Guo Loo! Wang Guo Loo!"* We tried to ignore them, but they wouldn't stop the chant.

Before I knew what was happening, I saw Father carrying a bucket of water and running to the gate. I followed behind to see him dashing the water at the Chinese boys. Repeated splashes of water forced the boys to scatter and the hateful chants finally stopped. But that wasn't to be the end. In a little while, I saw the boys returning accompanied by a French policeman. Except for the uniform, he wasn't really French; he was an Annamese or Indo-Chinese brought to Shanghai by the French to do their work as policemen just as the British brought the Sikhs from India to police the International Settlement.

We couldn't understand what the policeman was shouting about, but he quickly handcuffed both Father and me and marched us down the street with the victorious Chinese boys following behind and resuming their chant: *"Wang Guo Loo! Wang Guo Loo! Wang Guo Loo!"*

At the police station, we were thrown into a dungeon-like cell. I had never seen the inside of a jail, and its dark, damp, and putrid confines frightened me. A horrifying thought flashed through my mind; I might spend the rest of my life in this prison.

Father saw my fright. He came close to me, patted my head, and said, "Pedro-ya, don't be afraid. If you are not afraid, you can conquer anything." His firm hand, his comforting voice, and his fearless words calmed me and gave me strength.

"All right, Papa," I said. "I am not afraid." Still, I could not understand why we had been arrested and jailed. To comfort me and to pass the time, Father began telling me the biblical story of Daniel being thrown into a lion's den.

"But the lions didn't harm him," Father said, "because Daniel wasn't afraid of the lions." I knew the story of Daniel, but listening to Father telling it in the darkness of a Shanghai jail made it utterly real. I made up my mind to be like Daniel.

We were startled by the guard who opened the jail gate and led us up to the judge, a Frenchman. Through a Chinese interpreter, we were told that we had been arrested because we were beating little Chinese children. The policeman who had arrested us appeared to testify. I couldn't believe my eyes; he was wearing a uniform that was torn to shreds. His testimony was brief and terse; he went to the aid of children being beaten by the Korean father and son who attacked him and tore up his uniform. The judge, too, was brief and terse: guilty. Throw them in the cell. We were shoved back into the dungeon.

My first lesson in police frameup. Suddenly I was seized with hunger—I hadn't eaten all day! But how could I be hungry at such a time and in such a place? Yet I was famished. Will they feed us? Will they torture us? Will we ever get out of this filthy jail? All kinds of terrifying questions kept besieging me. Father held me close to him and began humming his favorite hymn: "Onward Christian soldiers, marching as to war. . . ." Then he kept assuring me, "We'll get out, Pedro-ya . . . we'll get out. . . ."

Chapter 9

I didn't know how much time had elapsed, but once again we were startled by the guard. He rattled the jail gate open and shouted, "Go home!" We groped out of the dungeon into the light, blinking. And there he was! Our savior! It was the young revolutionary and our faithful friend, Park Huen-Young! He apologized for having taken so long. He said that he had had a bit of trouble raising the necessary bribe money. Father thanked him and told him that he was sure Park would be the one to rescue us. We were free and relieved at last, but the pain of humiliation lingered in our hearts. The three of us walked home in depressing silence.

10

LITTLE
REVOLUTIONARIES

I BECAME A MEMBER of the Soh-Nyun Hyung-Myung Dan—the
Young Revolutionary Society. It was a secret club of boys, most of
whom were the sons of the leaders. Its major purpose was to "contrib-
ute to the Korean independence movement." All of us were only thirteen or fourteen years old, but we were deadly serious. Our pledge: To
be ready to sacrifice our lives, if necessary, for Korean independence, to
be fearless, and never to betray anyone. Our activities covered a wide
range—from all kinds of sports for strong bodies, to distributing leaflets for mass meetings, and, finally, to tracking down suspected spies
and traitors. We jealously guarded our secrets: names of members,
secret codes for special signals and messages, and, most important of
all, the amount of money in our treasury and where the money was
kept.

Of course, our fierce patriotism emanated from our parents, but it
was nurtured in the classrooms of In-Sung Hak-Kyo—the Wisdom
Building Learning Hall, an elementary school established by the revolutionaries to educate all Korean youth in Shanghai. Although I had
already graduated from the elementary school in Korea, I enrolled
because this was truly an independent Korean school. The subjects I
had already studied such as arithmetic and geography were taught with
new meaning and purpose. The school also taught subjects I had never

heard of in the Korean schools run by the Japanese. Now I learned for the first time about Korean art, Korean history, and Korean achievements. These studies at In-Sung imbued us with patriotism, and we learned to regard patriotism not only as a noble sentiment but also as a mission in life.

I discovered that the name "Korea" was given by the Westerners who first came in contact with the Koryu kingdom. But Korean history went back two thousand years before the Koryu period. According to legends and tradition, the first organized society in Korea was established in the year 2333 B.C. by the mythical figure known as Tan-Gun. Recorded history began with a group of refugees from China led by Ki-Ja who settled in Korea in the year 1122 B.C. With the artisans and scholars he brought with him, Ki-Ja established the first Korean kingdom and called it Chosun: Kingdom of Morning Calm. My own family ancestors are believed to have accompanied Ki-Ja from China. Ki-Ja and his followers taught the primitive people of Korea how to cultivate the land, to obtain food from the river and the sea, to better clothe and house themselves, and to learn the letters of China.

Out of such beginnings, some thousand years later, the Koreans developed a powerful kingdom known as Koguryo. It covered all of northern Korea as well as vast areas of Manchuria. It had a thriving agricultural economy supplemented by raising livestock, fishing, and hunting. It had already generated the bronze and the iron cultures. Its government was organized into branches, each one responsible for its assigned special duties, and it also formulated codes of law, morals, and religion. Their military prowess was so great they not only repulsed the Mongol and Chinese invaders but conducted their own conquest of outlying Chinese colonies.

Simultaneously during this period, two other centers of civilization had developed: one in the southeastern region known as Silla, and the other in the southwestern region called Paekche. Together with Koguryo, the kingdoms of Silla and Paekche are known as the "Three Kingdoms" in Korean history. The kingdom of Paekche was rather short-lived, but it left a lasting mark especially in its relations with Japan. It was this Paekche kingdom that sent its artisans and craftsmen to Japan to teach the islanders. In A.D. 285 Paekche dispatched to Japan groups of brewers, tailors, tile-makers, and ceramicists who helped to invigorate Japan's own culture. Moreover, at the behest of the Japanese emperor, a famous Korean scholar named Wang-In, whom the Japanese called Wa-Ni, was sent to teach Chinese classics to the royalty. The Paekche kingdom was hedonistically inclined, however, and rapidly became decadent and fell to the dominant power of Silla in A.D. 600. Then allied with the newly rising T'ang dynasty of China, Silla also overpowered Koguryo and brought the entire peninsula under unified rule. The Silla kingdom flourished for centuries in what was known as the "Golden Age."

Toward the end of its nearly thousand-year rule, Silla fell victim to the feuds of its own overlords. Wang-Keun overwhelmed the rest and seized power to rule the kingdom. In A.D. 1231 the Mongols came. The lives of thousands of Koreans and a measureless amount of material were sacrificed for Genghis Khan's ambitious but futile adventures.

The Mongols were eventually forced to depart from Korea, and the wasted kingdom then fell victim to the domination of Buddhist monks and priests who used their influence to direct all state affairs. Out of the confusion and chaos, General Lee Sung-Gae revolted and took over the reins of the kingdom. It was the beginning of the Yi (Lee) dynasty, the last Korean kingdom, which ruled for five hundred years until its conquest in 1910 by the "Sons of the Rising Sun," the Japanese.

My two years at the In-Sung school in Shanghai and the studies in Korean arts and history reshaped me as a true Korean: patriotic and proud, no longer ashamed of the kind of life I had lived in Korea under the Japanese rulers. The history lessons they taught at In-Sung were so vivid that I actually lived through all the glorious adventures, the exquisite exploits in arts, and the horrifying wars against the invaders. I identified with the great heroes and heroines, with the great artists and scholars. Throughout the long history, each dynasty left its own rich and distinct imprint: Koguryo, its art of war; Silla, its beautiful temples and pagodas; and Koryu, the flower of Buddhism and its famous celadon porcelain.

The Yi dynasty, too, had its struggles against foreign invaders: the Japanese from the south and the Manchus from the north. Hideyoshi sought to use Korea as a stepping stone for the conquest of Manchuria and China in 1592. But his dreams were shattered by the famous

Korean patriot Admiral Lee Soon-Shin. With his fleet of armored Turtle Ships, Admiral Lee engaged and sank most of the Japanese fleet. Of course, Admiral Lee Soon-Shin became my hero, and I dreamed that someday I too would rid Korea of Japanese oppressors.

The defeat of the Japanese forces under Hideyoshi was soon followed by attacks of the Manchus from the north. They overran most of northern Korea and laid siege to Seoul. With devastation across the country and the capture of multitudes of people as slaves, Korea was forced to accept the Manchus' suzerainty. Such repeated disillusionments in dealing with foreign powers finally led the kings to seal the borders and avoid all contact with the outside world. Korea thus earned its sobriquet, the "Hermit Kingdom."

In spite of the deliberate isolation, the Yi dynasty made remarkable progress. It instituted a system of public education, introduced civil examinations for government offices, humanized the treatment of criminals, and devised a more equitable method of taxation. It was in this period, fifty years before Gutenberg, that a Korean invented the movable type which gave birth to a great upsurge in the publication of literary classics. Another remarkable achievement was the development of the Korean phonetic alphabet by scholars. Until then, the Chinese classics were the only available texts of learning and only a select group of privileged people could afford them. The phonetic alphabet changed all this and literacy became the general rule, rather than the exception it had been. The alphabet, possibly more than any other single factor, was responsible for the formation of a unified national identity of the Korean people. Oh, how proud I was to learn the origin of the Korean written language called Gook-Moon—the National Letters.

My study of Korean history then reached modern times. The national isolationism imposed by the kings of the Yi dynasty did not deter the covetous designs of the surrounding nations: China, Russia, and Japan. In 1876, Japan forced a trade treaty on Korea followed by a similar treaty in 1882 with the United States. The latter treaty, however, contained a mutual pledge of aid in the event of attack by a foreign power. The ever intensifying rivalry for the control of Korea ultimately resulted in the Sino-Japanese war in 1894 followed by the Russo-Japanese war in 1904. Victorious in both wars, Japan proclaimed itself the sole "protector" of Korea. Korea evoked its treaty with the United States and appealed for help. President Theodore Roosevelt brushed the appeal aside and advised the Koreans to "cooperate with Japan." It was not by accident that the peace treaty between Russia and Japan was signed at Portsmouth, New Hampshire. With such encouragement, Japan abandoned all pretext and annexed Korea in 1910. I was then four years old.

Now for the first time, at age fourteen, I was learning the history and the rich heritage of my country. To devote our lives to regain freedom and independence was the central theme of every subject we studied at the In-Sung school in Shanghai. The Young Revolutionary Society was the natural outgrowth of our learning. All its members were sons of exiled Korean revolutionaries. Among them were the sons of two famous patriots: Phillip Kim, the son of the foreign minister, Dr. Kim Kiu-Sik, and Ahn Won-Sang, the son of Korean martyr Ahn Jung-Gun. It was he who assassinated Prince Ito, the first Japanese governor sent to Korea by the emperor.

As a special dispensation, we accepted two girls as members of our society: Park Hai-Yung—"Daughter of the Sea"—for her extraordinary beauty and Chai Ok-Nyuh—"Daughter of Jade"—for her extraordinary brains. They were startlingly different, not only physically but in spirit. Hai-Yung, the daughter of a Korean refugee family from Vladivostok, was a beautiful girl with a bubbling good humor. She laughed loudly at everyone's jokes and all the boys vied for her attention. Of completely different makeup was Ok-Nyuh, the daughter of a minor official in the movement. She was unusually skinny and shy, and her nearsightedness made her squint. However, her appearance was forgotten when she spoke. We all admired her brilliant mind, and at examination time the boys always sought her help! Both girls were great assets to our club.

Our patriotic zeal and revolutionary spirit did not keep us from being very young at heart. We were forever searching for enjoyment: sports, dramatics, and watching girls. Yes, our heads were with the independence movement but our hearts always strayed for fun and play. We composed our songs and wrote our plays and performed them as entertainment at the political gatherings of our elders. They were enthusiastic about our performances and encouraged us to do more.

In summer, we played baseball. By adding some younger boys to play with us, we managed to form a Korean baseball team and practiced daily to develop our skill and confidence. Soon the caliber of our team was tested against teams of Chinese schools. We were surprisingly good and beat them regularly, and we celebrated each victory by going to the noodle shop. Baseball was rather new to the Chinese, and they were not particularly fond of the game. So we began looking for better competition. Someone thought of playing the American school; being Americans, we thought, they should give us good enough competition. The challenge was made and a certain Saturday afternoon was set for the match. The entire Korean community became involved and a large number of parents and friends turned out to watch the game. And to our surprise, even some of the Chinese student whom we had defeated so often showed up to see the contest.

It was a disaster! We were simply no match for the Americans; they outplayed us at every position and in every phase. Indeed, we discovered the gross disparity the first time we went to bat. We had never seen the ball traveling at such speed. The American pitcher kept striking us out or at best tossing us out with weak dribblers. But when they came to bat, it was monotonous—hit after booming hit. Even our best pitcher could not silence their bats. The final score at the end of a long day was something we chose not to remember. Nor was it any consolation to discover later that the team we had challenged was the champion American High School team. It was the first and the last baseball game we played against the Americans!

We did much better with soccer. Koreans naturally took to it— from early childhood, we used our feet and kicking for different kinds of games and as our chief weapons in fighting. For lack of boys, however, the Korean soccer team included a few older men, and I played right wing. The Chinese found their traditional training in the martial arts very suitable to soccer, as well. So whenever the Koreans and the Chinese played soccer, it invariably exploded into a battle royal, usually resulting in victory or defeat by a single goal, or sometimes even a tie. And we gained some measure of satisfaction when the American High School refused to accept our challenge in soccer.

For us, the members of the "Secret Society," a victory in soccer meant a great deal more than just winning a game. It meant that we were strong and able to uphold the honor of our country. A win at soccer always raised our spirits, and our celebration at the noodle shop would be noisier than ever. And when we met again at the meeting of our society, the singing of our national anthem reverberated with greater zeal and emotion:

> Three thousand *li* of mu-gung blossoms
> Clothe the beautiful mountains and rivers.
> Korea by the Koreans,
> Shall be preserved forever.

About this time, our close-knit circle was disturbed by an unusual distraction. A Russian émigré family moved into one of the apartments in the compound where some of our members lived. This neighborhood was our favorite gathering place and we spent much of our time there practicing baseball on the street. The distraction was that the new Russian family had a daughter of our age whose beauty was breathtaking. Even now I remember her vividly, in the flowing white dress she always wore, sitting at the little balcony overlooking the street where we played. Every afternoon, day after day, the beauty appeared on the balcony like an apparition. To our young hearts that was terribly distracting, but we dared not show our admiration because a very large, elderly woman sat behind the young lady, watching. It was a tantalizing mystery which was partly answered one day when one boy in our group, who spoke fluent Russian, brought the news that the angelic beauty was really a Russian Princess and the large woman her guardian. This bit of news made the daily afternoon scene on the balcony all the more intriguing. Now I had a formidable challenge: I had to get to know this Princess. But how?

The baseball season over, it was now roller-skating time. As soon as school ended, I would hurry to the house with the balcony, put on my skates, and glide back and forth like a peacock showing off its plumage. Yes, I could tell the Princess was fascinated and I thought I even detected a faint smile now and then. Through my Russian-speaking friend, I smuggled an idea to the guardian: she should buy a pair of skates for the Princess and come to the park, and I would be happy to teach her how to skate. A few days later as I was parading on my skates before her, I saw the Princess faintly nodding and smiling at me. I almost ran into a tree! I guessed and I hoped that her signals were to let me know that she got my message or that she had gotten the skates. Just then, the guardian momentarily left her station. Seizing the opportunity, I quickly stopped under the balcony, looked up, and smiled. And the Princess responded with a most heartwarming smile. Soon afterwards, while my heart was still throbbing, my Russian-speaking friend brought more exciting news: the Princess has her skates, he said, and she would be at the park on the coming Saturday afternoon.

To meet the Princess in person, to talk with her, and perhaps even touch her! I thought that Saturday would never come. Of course I was the first one at the park that afternoon. I hardly noticed the usual crowd of boys and girls gathering at the skating rink. The only thing on my mind was, "Will she come? Will she really come?" Then in a flash, there she was! The Princess was gracefully walking toward me with her guardian following close behind. I moved toward her as in a dream and motioned her to sit on the bench so I could help put on her skates. I don't remember what language I spoke: Korean, Chinese, Pidgin English, or just plain nervous pantomime. No matter, she understood me and I understood her Russian.

In a stern tone of voice, the guardian spoke to the Princess who then sat on the bench and fixed the skates by herself. Obviously she had done it before, and she had also learned how to skate, though not very well. I followed close by and at every opportunity reached out to hold her arm and give her support. At each such moment, she would turn her head and reward me with a heavenly smile. Encouraged, I grasped her hand and began skating by her side. All my friends stopped skating and stared at us with open mouths. I could hear them whispering, "Look, look at Peter! Look at him!" Soon, I taught the Princess to cross her hands while I crossed mine, and holding each other's hands, we floated around the rink. I put my arm around her waist and held her as closely as I dared. Oh, how soft and warm she felt! For a long time thereafter, I relived that blissful afternoon skating with a Russian Princess.

One of the major undertakings of our society was raising money to support all the activities. For this purpose, we presented entertainment programs at the meetings of the leaders. We'd make up and perform a new show at each such gathering, and we would be rewarded with a generous donation. We also staged our own parties and invited families and friends. There was no charge for admission, of course, but at the end of our program we always remembered to take up a collection. The varying amounts of money indicated how well our program was received. From the days of the Sunday School in Korea, I always enjoyed performing. I loved the feeling of people responding to what I said and did on the stage. Since coming to Shanghai, the main parts of my performances were impersonations and imitations, my subjects varying from the revolutionary leaders to American movie stars. And I created and directed all the entertainment programs.

In time, I developed a repertoire of my own. Among the more popular numbers were my impersonations of the Shanghai policemen: Sikhs, Annamese (Indo-Chinese), French, and British. For the climax, all of them would appear at the same time, to argue and fight to claim a prisoner. The audience also enjoyed my imitations of our own leaders—all making fiery political speeches, each in his distinct and peculiar style. The most artistic number, they thought, was my imitation of Charlie Chaplin! It was suggested that we should hold a theatre night: an evening's entertainment without political speeches.

We welcomed the idea and soon staged our first evening of theatre. I made up the program in two parts: musicals and skits. The musical numbers were really various nationalities singing other people's songs: the Korean singing an American song and vice versa, the Japanese singing Chinese songs, and so on. I sang an American song in gibberish as it is sung in a church, in an opera, and in a dance hall. The skits dealt with the most unlikely happenings in the Korean community: Korean elders learning to play baseball and roller skating, Charlie Chaplin visiting the Korean community and discovering Korean foods and customs, and other such incongruous scenes.

Such were the kinds of activities of my youth that kindled my serious interest in the theatre. No one knew what dreams I had, and I wouldn't confide in anyone for fear of being ridiculed. To be an actor? Unthinkable! Why, an actor was an outcast with no status or respect in society. Being allowed to hold an evening of theatre was only an indulgence, encouraging the youth to spend their time on "good wholesome entertainment." In any case, there was no place to go to study the theatre. The only available sources were the Chinese opera and the movies. But from both I learned a great deal about how to make people laugh, to intensify their interest, and to arouse excitement. In preparing the society's dramatic programs, I relied chiefly on my theatrical instincts and the lessons from my performing experiences.

I was sixteen when I wrote my first play; it was called *The Lovers*. I assembled a cast which included some college graduates from Japan, directed the rehearsals, rented a large church auditorium, and presented the play to a capacity audience. Here is the outline of the play.

Act I: A young boy and a young girl are sitting on a park bench. They are deeply in love. He gazes at her and sighs; she gazes at him and sighs; they gaze at each other and sigh together. Many boisterous scenes then take place near and around the bench: an old lady argues with a vendor about the wretched cakes he sold her, someone runs in and hides behind the bench followed by a group of policemen who blame each other for losing the criminal, screaming children run around the bench playing a game of catch, and so on. To all this commotion, the two lovers are oblivious. They are content only to gaze at each other and sigh.

Act II: The lovers, now married, are in their home. The scene is the living room which separates two other rooms on either side. A loud and angry voice is heard from one room. In response, an angry woman's voice comes out of the other room. The man sticks his head out and shakes his fist at the other room. It's the young lover. He derides his wife for the horrible food, the missing buttons, and the dust on his desk. He shakes his fist once more, slams the door, and disappears. The wife appears out of the other room. She is disheveled and carries an old broom. She shakes the broom in anger and retorts how filthy and gross he is when he is drunk, how sloppy with his clothes, how stingy with his money. She throws the broom down and runs back to her room.

The husband reappears, draws a line with chalk across the room, and declares war. He says, "From now on, you stay on your side and I'll stay on mine. Don't you ever cross this line without my permission." He sits on the floor and begins to read a book. The wife enters carrying a garment she is sewing. As she sits on the floor and begins to sew, she says, "That's a very good idea. Now, I don't have to worry about anything." Time passes in silence but soon some problems arise: husband is thirsty but he can't cross the line to go to the kitchen; wife needs her sewing box left in the other room but dares not cross the line. Only pantomime and gestures indicate their frustration. Long silence. The heat of anger seems to dissipate. Husband clears his throat and bravely addresses his wife, "Don't you want to come over to my side?" Wife shakes her head and answers nonchalantly, "No, but if you want to come over to my side. . . ."

Act III: A year later in the same home. The dividing line is gone; peace and tranquillity pervade the air. The husband, sitting in his usual place, is still reading. And the wife, in her usual place, is sitting and sewing. They seem like complete strangers. Husband looks longingly at the wife and coughs loudly as a signal for his hunger. Wife goes out and shortly returns with a little table which she sets down on the floor. Husband takes the table and ravenously eats his dinner. He spills some soup and helplessly looks at his wife who does not pay any attention. Husband walks out, returns with a mop, and cleans the floor. He finishes his dinner with a loud belch (an old Korean custom) which means he has finished. Wife takes the table and eats what is left (another ancient Korean custom).

Husband speaks as though to himself, "There is a very good movie at our neighborhood theatre. . . ." Then the wife also speaks, as though to herself, "I don't mind going to see it. . . ." Both retire to their rooms and reappear shortly, dressed for an evening at the theatre. Their transformation is stunning. But the husband pretends not to notice. He looks into space and utters, "My, what a beautiful lady!" The wife mimics her husband, looks into space in the opposite direction, and murmurs, "Why, what a handsome gentleman!"

The audience's reception was beyond all my hopes. Of course they were all friendly and sympathetic people, but I thought the guffaws and bursts of laughter were genuine. This first full-blown venture— writing, directing, and producing—was full of faults, crudities, and many amateurish mishaps. But the very weakness, our innocence and naivete, made everything happening on stage believable. These theatricals of my youth were gratifying and fun. What I did not suspect was that this emotional gravitation toward the theatre would abide with me for the rest of my life. It would lay dormant for many years, but at the first opportunity, and with the slightest incentive, it would resurface.

About this time, I learned that the first Chinese film group was forming in Shanghai and planning to make the first Chinese movie. I found their office and talked to several people for a possible job. They said that they would get in touch with me when their plans were more definite. I never heard from them.

Two years had flown by since our arrival in China and our happy reunion with Father. The vast city of Shanghai with its endless fascination was now my home; I was a part of its throbbing millions. Within this complex metropolis, the tiny Korean commmunity kept alive its identity, its special mission. But undoubtedly there were other little circles with their own national identities and interests. The In-Sung school was unique and served only the needs of the Koreans. There were other little schools throughout the city, each serving the cultural and religious as well as the political and financial interests of its own community. This complexity and diversity formed the very heart of Shanghai.

Now my graduation from In-Sung was approaching. The two years of study there gave me much enlightenment and helped to crystallize my identification as a Korean; they were the most valuable two years of my life. But who could have known that only a few days before graduation, an undreamed-of storm would break over my head! The nature of the outbreak was serious enough to threaten my graduation. A girl was the storm center. She was a young refugee from Vladivostok named Luva. Luva didn't attend In-Sung, for she was much older than we were, but she often dropped in at our school to visit her friend Hai-Yung, who too had come from Russia. Luva was a voluptuous girl, and she loved the attention she received. Moreover, she was fun-loving, boisterous, and outgoing. And somehow she always managed to provoke some hilarious incidents among the students.

One afternoon, I had the job of delivering an important message to a man who happened to be living at Luva's house. When I arrived there and knocked at the door, it was Luva who opened it. Seeing me looking surprised and flustered, she beamed and invited me in. I told her I was bringing a message for the man living there. Ignoring what I said, she again asked me to come in the house. She laughed at my hesitation, and growing impatient, seized my arm and pulled me in. She offered me a seat and laughed merrily at my apparent nervousness. It dawned on me that the man I was to contact was not in; in fact, there was no one else in the house besides Luva. I pleaded that I had to return with the undelivered message and started toward the door. Like lightning, Luva grabbed me from behind, spun me around, and began kissing me. I was totally unprepared and I was helpless. It seemed she was kissing me on my mouth for a long time before releasing me and laughing in triumph. I dashed out of the house and ran. According to all the Korean teachings, I was disgraced. But how much, I didn't know. Nor could I have anticipated the even more disgraceful aftermath.

The next day in school, there was a strange atmosphere around me. Everywhere I went, I noticed the furtive glances, the abrupt halt of conversations, and the seemingly irrepressible giggles. To get at the root of it all, I grabbed a boy and demanded to know what the joke was about.

"They say . . . ," he stuttered.

"All right, they say what?"

"They say . . . ," the boy mumbled, "that you went to Luva's house yesterday."

"So, what's so funny about that?"

"They say . . . ," the boy began stuttering again, "that you grabbed Luva . . . and hugged her . . . and kissed her . . . HARD." But despite my threats he wouldn't tell me who had told him such a story. So, that was it! But how did the story spread so fast and get so distorted? It had to be Luva herself. Flushed with triumph, she had to dash to her friend and tell her own version of my visit. I had to put a stop to this scandalous disgrace. But how?

At the lunch recess when the joke was in full bloom, I picked out the biggest boy who was also somewhat of a bully; his name was Choi. I went up to him and called out, "Choi! Did you tell everybody I kissed Luva?" He looked away and burst into laughter. "Listen, Choi," I said loud enough for everyone to hear, "you'd better apologize. If you don't, I'll fight you." Boys and girls began gathering around us while Choi kept laughing. Suddenly he stopped laughing, lowered his head, and charged. A true North Korean, he fought by butting with his head! Yes, I had heard how boys in Pyongyang, the ancient capital in the north, were trained from early childhood to fight with their heads. A little pebble would be tied and suspended at the gate, and the boy had to knock the stone with his head each time he entered or left the house. As he grew, the size of the stone also grew until his head became as hard as the rock. I had also heard the story of a Pyongyang man who, in a fight, cracked open the head of a Japanese adversary. When the two were hauled into court, the judge asked the Japanese victim what kind of weapon the Korean had used.

"He butted me with his head," the Japanese answered.

"Well, in that case," the judge said, "it must have hurt him as much as it hurt you. Case dismissed."

So I knew better; I wouldn't let him butt me, especially in the head. Instantly I stepped aside and, at the same time, delivered a swift kick to his leg. I let him know that I was from the south where we were trained to fight with our legs and feet. Choi stumbled but did not fall. He straightened and charged again. The boys and girls circling us laughed and clapped, but as the fight grew deadly serious, they stopped laughing. In another fierce charge, Choi found his target: my head. I felt dizzy and almost fell. In desperation, I leaped high and kicked. My foot caught his chin and he began to spit blood. I was hoping he would fall so that I could kick him until he begged for mercy and apologized. But the struggle went on until both of us were tiring and panting. Then, suddenly, all the boys and girls scattered and disappeared, and I heard the teacher's voice: "Stop! Stop! Stop the fight!"

Choi and I froze in our tracks. The teacher looked even angrier than we were. "Both of you," he could hardly speak, "come to the office. Right now!" He turned, leaving us to follow him. We walked upstairs and entered the waiting room, still seething with anger. The teacher first called Choi into the office and shut the door. Wondering what would happen to Choi, my anger subsided. Momentarily, I heard the sharp crackling of the whip. Of course, Choi was being given the traditional Korean punishment: whipping on bare legs with a dry reed. I heard repeated whistles of the reed and its sharp cracks on the bare skin, and I began to worry. When the whipping finally stopped and

Choi emerged from the office, I was amazed to see his face; there was no trace of tears or pain.

Then I heard the teacher's call. I braced myself and entered the office. Without a word, the teacher gestured for me to stand against the wall and roll up the pants over my legs. I peered over my shoulder and saw the teacher flexing a fresh batch of reeds. In that instant, the whipping scene in Korea flashed through my mind. But then it was a Japanese teacher who administered the whipping, for insulting the Japanese emperor. Here, this was in Shanghai, in a free Korean school and a Korean teacher. Why should he resort to whipping? It was puzzling.

"*Ee-nom-ah!* Stupid one!" The teacher called out and punctuated it with the reed whistling and cracking on my bare legs. I winced to hold back the tears.

"*Ee-nom-ah!*" Another whistle, another crack! He kept whipping and I stopped counting; the stinging pain was becoming unbearable. Then something strange happened; the teacher began reciting bitterly while continuing the whipping.

"You are a Korean." *Crack!* "Not South Korean—just Korean!" *Crack!* His words were more stinging than his whip. "Choi is also a Korean!" *Crack!* "Not North Korean!" *Crack!* "Just Korean!" *Crack!* "Do you understand that?" *Crack!* "The Japanese conquered us because we were divided!" *Crack!* The whipping stopped momentarily, and I turned and saw the teacher in tears.

"If you hate Choi because he is from the north, and he hates you because you are from the south. . . ." He could hardly control himself, and weakly he swung the reed across my legs. "Then there's no hope for the Koreans!" He threw the reed away, went to his desk, and slumped over it. He was sobbing, "There's no hope! There's no hope! We'll always be slaves!" Without even lifting his head, he blurted, "Leave the room!"

I walked out in a daze; I was stunned. I had never seen a man crying, let alone before a boy, and I had never witnessed such agonizing pain on a man's face. With the whipping, the teacher taught me a most valuable lesson, and I vowed to remember it always.

The teacher could very well have used the incident as sufficient reason to prevent my graduation, but he didn't. I was thankful, and my respect and admiration for the teacher rose tenfold. The teacher beamed with pride as he watched us at the commencement. We were the first class to graduate from the independent Korean school: two boys and two girls. Everyone made a speech. Mine was about Korean independence through unity of its people. In the evening, there was a celebration honoring the graduates. We were made to feel that the entire burden of regaining Korean independence rested on our shoulders. There were more speeches by the elders, but soon all the somberness gave way to fun and laughter. The elders regaled us with funny stories, singing and reciting newly composed poems. Eventually, of course, I was asked to do my imitation of the Shanghai policemen. No elementary school graduates could have been more honored, not only by the parents and faculty but also by the leaders of the Korean revolutionary movement.

The great honor heaped on us at the commencement and our soaring pride and confidence gradually dissipated during the summer that followed. We met at the park every day as usual, but there was no fun and little laughter. We were conscious of what was happening, but we were helpless to stop the depression that was engulfing us. Our central concern was our future. We all had a burning desire to obtain a higher education, but no one knew how. There was no secondary Korean school, so we would have to attend a Chinese high school. But where and with what means? We were all discouraged and lost interest even in the new baseball season. Our spirits seemed to fade away just like the Russian Princess who moved from the area and was never to be seen again on that little balcony. We loafed around in the park, and when the sun began to set, we would adjourn to one of our friend's homes and pass away the evening. The only solace we had were a few cool summer melons which we would share to stave off the gloom and the summer heat.

Just when our spirits were lowest, a young Chinese man appeared on the scene to drive our depression even deeper. Although apparently without work, he was always dressed in a rich silk tunic and loitered around our friends' neighborhood. We were told that he was a member of a notorious and powerful gang. The first time he saw us, he called out, "Hey! *Wang Guo Loo! Wang Guo Loo!*" "Lost country slaves! Lost country slaves!" It was the most hateful curse anyone could hurl at us. Every afternoon, he would station himself across the street from our friend's home and wait. And at the first sight of us, he would begin the taunting: *"Wang Guo Loo! Wang Guo Loo!"* Ignoring him, we would walk on, but he would keep chanting to accompany our footsteps. It was insufferable but we were helpless, for we were warned that a Chinese gangster always carried a weapon under his silk tunic.

One evening the inevitable finally happened, and that was the day when I was not with the group. An emergency messenger came running to our home in great excitement. The message was for me: "Flee! Flee immediately! Don't spend the night at home! Get out of Shanghai!" With such a message, no questions were asked. Umma packed some of my clothes in Father's little suitcase, and together we rushed off to the Shanghai railway station. She bought a one-way ticket to Nanking and put me on the train. I was also given a letter hastily written by Father and addressed to an American living in Nanking.

Upon arrival there, I found the Chinese high school called Jung-Wha Gung Sho, "Great China Middle Academy." It was established by American missionaries whose principal was an American woman named Miss Probesco. I found her office and presented Father's letter to her. She read it quickly, then rushed over to shake my hand. That was how I found myself in another strange city attending a Chinese high school. But the emergency message, the order to flee Shanghai, remained a mystery until I had finished the school year and returned home. I met my classmate Ahn Joon-Sang who told me the full story.

On that fateful day, the Young Revolutionaries had spent the day in the park as usual. When the sun began to set, they headed for the usual friend's house for the evening. On their way they bought a large watermelon for the evening's refreshment. As they approached, they spotted the Chinese gangster waiting for them. Leaning against the wall with folded arms, he began his chant: *"Wang Guo Loo! Wang Guo Loo! Wang Guo Loo!"* Of course, everyone heard him but no one said a word. The gangster kept up the chant with a special fervor that day, and it could still be heard when they retreated into the house.

They put the melon on the table and brought a kitchen knife and cut it up, but no one was interested in eating. The gangster was still out there, still bellowing the degrading epithet, loudly enough for them to hear it in the house.

"Let's go get him!" Someone spat out the words everyone was thinking.

"Yes, let's go get him!" The response was unanimous. They dropped the melon and rushed out.

The gangster was startled to see the young Korean boys rushing at him from all sides. Gangsters were reputed to be experts in the Chinese martial arts. He struck his stance, prepared to do battle. He leaped and flailed his arms and fists with ferocious grunts. What he was not aware of was that he was facing "Young Revolutionaries" who were ready to offer their lives for the honor of their country. The gangster knocked some boys down, but they rose and rushed back. Some of them applied their bone-breaking heads and butted him while others kicked from all sides. The surging anger and bitter hatred of the young Koreans finally felled the gangster.

"Hey! He's bleeding!" someone cried out. The gangster was lying limp in a pool of blood. Everyone scattered. The man might have lived if the mob that gathered had not lifted the wounded body and paraded around the street shouting: "Look! Look! They killed him! They killed him!"

Anticipating retaliation from the gangsters, the emergency messengers were dispatched to warn everyone, including me, to leave the city. When I heard this account of the fateful evening, I felt that I should have been there, too. Of course, I didn't ask Ahn who carried the kitchen knife to the fight, and to this day, no one has asked or knows who plunged the knife into the tormentor's chest.

Miss Probesco, the principal, was a tall and handsome lady. Even though I was late for registration and I didn't have the money on hand for the tuition, she allowed me to attend the classes. She assigned me to a room to share with another student, and in every way made me feel at home and welcome. Overnight, I became a full-fledged student in a Chinese high school, living in a dormitory with a hundred other Chinese students. The school was housed in a two-story brick building: upstairs for the dormitory and downstairs for classrooms, except one separate room near the school entrance which served as Miss Probesco's office.

All the teachers, except Mr. Smith who taught English, were Chinese. Naturally, all the academic subjects such as algebra, biology, and history were taught in Chinese. So, for the second time in my life, I had to change my language completely; first from Korean to Japanese, and now to Chinese. But for the education I wanted, I had no choice but to adopt Chinese as my own language. I was gratified that after a few months of struggle I was able to follow most of the lessons in classes. In fact, toward the end of the school year I became quite proficient both in spoken and written Chinese, and the teachers and the students accepted me as one of them.

But the study of English was another matter. Mr. Smith, the American teacher, gave each student a strange textbook. With it we studied the alphabet—the strange tongue-twisting sounds of the letters and the many winding and circling ways of writing them. Compared to Korean and Chinese, and even to Japanese, the English language seemed to have no logic at all. The simple names such as dog, cat, and bird were difficult enough to learn, but when it came to their movements, it was utterly confusing: run, ran, run; go, went, gone; fly, flew, flown. In Chinese, the verb was always the same and the tenses were denoted by the juxtaposition of time: run today, run yesterday, run tomorrow; go today, go yesterday, go tomorrow; fly today, fly yesterday, fly tomorrow, perfectly logical and easily understood.

A more serious problem in school, however, was not in the classroom but in the dining room. I never had enough to eat and I was perpetually hungry. We had three meals a day: breakfast at seven, lunch at twelve, and dinner at six. When the bell rang, a hundred students would dash into the dining hall and take their seats at large square tables, eight to each table. The kitchen helpers carried in pots and platters of food and set them on the tables. For breakfast, it was rice gruel and fried curls—straight donuts; for lunch, rice with a vegetable and a meat dish; and for supper, rice with two vegetables and two meat dishes, or sometimes a fish dish. When the food was placed on all the tables, a teacher offered grace.

"Amen" was the signal for the hungry students to dive in. It was a race; the faster one ate, the more he ate. The Chinese students were all masters of the art which called for elimination of all unnecessary movements and concentration on the basics. Hold the rice bowl in the left hand and bring it up to your mouth. Hold the chopsticks in the right hand and deftly shovel the rice into your mouth. At any cost, do not stop shoveling! The only interruption was to pick up a piece of meat or vegetable quickly to spice the rice. Through the entire meal, nothing but the chopsticks and the mouths moved. When the rice bowl was emptied, it took no more than three seconds to refill the bowl with rice and resume the action. For the Chinese student, it took less than two minutes to finish a bowl of rice, and when they had all eaten four bowls, the table was picked clean except for some rice in the tub—barely eight minutes after "Amen."

From my earliest childhood, I was always scolded for being a slow eater, hardly a qualification to sit down at a table with Chinese students and engage in the daily race for life. No matter how hard I tried—gulping my food only half-chewed—I could not get a fair share of food. When everyone was finishing his fourth bowl of rice, I was barely starting on my second. Something had to be done to stave off the constant gnawing hunger. Fortunately I found an inexpensive solution. Whenever Umma sent me a little money, I would go to the store and buy a jar of preserved tofu—salted beancurd—which I would take with me to the dining room. When the Chinese students finished eating and the table had been picked clean, I would open my precious jar of salted tofu. And because there was always some left-over rice, I could sit alone and leisurely eat three more bowls of rice, spiced with tofu.

That was how I survived. But I was fifteen and growing, and the pain of hunger never really left me. The little money I occasionally received from Umma was invariably spent on food. I would invite a friend and together we would go to the town teahouse for a celebration, a feast. The teahouse was only a mud-floored shack where the laborers gathered to spend a penny or two, sip the hot tea, and rest their weary bones. But for those who could afford it, for ten pennies one could get six fried dumplings with the pot of tea. My friend and I would each devour twelve of those dumplings. I never knew what they were made of, but I had never eaten anything so delicious. What's more, for a few days at least, I was free of hunger pains.

Another problem, though not as constant as hunger, was spending the winter nights in my unheated dormitory room. In contrast to Shanghai, the winter in Nanking was frigid, and my first winter there we had three feet of snow. There was no heating of any kind in the entire school building. The frozen classrooms were just bearable during the day, for I did quick exercises between classes and then played soccer when the classes were over. But I dreaded the night when the bell rang for bedtime. Before the lights were turned off, I had to prepare myself for the ordeal of going to bed. The bed was a wooden bunk with a thin cotton mattress and a thin cotton blanket. The preparation began with piling all my books and every other portable object at the foot and the sides of the blanket. The only things I shed before going to bed were my shoes and the school jacket, all of which went on top of the blanket. All other clothing including pants stayed on me. Then I slid into the "sleeping tunnel," being very careful not to disturb the books and other objects piled on top of the blanket. It was like entering an ice tunnel until my body generated enough heat to warm it and allow me to fall asleep. When the spring brought the warming sun, I could feel my whole body thawing slowly. Finally, when the thawing was complete, all my toenails fell off!

My Nanking school days were not always so dreary. On the contrary, most of the days were filled with fun and excitement and I was happy. Indeed, my glowing report of Jung-Wha Middle Academy brought a group of other Koreans to enroll. With the Korean students as the nucleus, we formed a soccer team. After many hours of practice, we tested our skills and strength against other middle schools in the city. We were surprised and elated to discover we could beat all the high school teams in Nanking; we even became known as the "Ferocious Koreans." Then, toward the end of the winter semester, we received a challenge from a totally unknown school. It came from a middle school in a riverport town five hundred *li* north of Nanking. Miss Probesco gave us permission, and her blessing, to leave the school on a Friday, play the game on Saturday, and return on Sunday. This soccer match would not have materialized had it not been for the Korean students who were so enthused that they raised all the money needed for the team's boat fare.

We boarded a little steamboat early in the morning. It was a beautiful day and all through the long boat ride up the Yangtse River, we sang Korean revolutionary songs as though we were on our way to fight for Korean independence. Even some of the Chinese members of the team, who had heard these songs often and were appreciative of our emotional exuberance, joined us by loudly humming the tunes. Upon our arrival late in the afternoon, we were met by a deputation from the host school. We were taken to their dormitory in order to rest and recuperate from the long journey. But we were too excited to rest. Instead, we spent the time making up jokes and laughing hilariously about the country bumpkin soccer players. We were wagering with each other as to how many goals we would score.

Loud ringing of the dinner bell abruptly halted our bantering. We were ushered into the dining hall filled with the familiar square tables, eight to each table. But the food we were served was a great surprise. It turned out to be a feast. The kitchen helpers kept bringing dish after dish: several kinds of soup, roast duck, steamed fish, and a variety of vegetable dishes cooked with beef, pork, or chicken. There was no need to race through this meal. There was so much food, all so delicious, we relaxed and dined like rich gentlemen at a banquet. It was an unforgettable eating experience. Little did we suspect that there was to be another unforgettable event in store for us on the playing field the next day.

Saturday afternoon was a perfect day for soccer: clear sunny sky, crisp and invigorating air. We got our first surprise when we trotted onto the field; it was completely encircled by spectators. Evidently, the town had declared a holiday and the entire populace turned out to watch the game. Their loud applauding and hollering quickly dispelled our preconceived ideas of a country town. This was a *soccer* town. And when the game got under way, very quickly and effortlessly, the country bumpkins scored. The townspeople exploded with yells and screams. We held a quick huddle and decided we had better go to work. As we began to charge, the country team stepped up its pace and scored another goal. Another outburst from the townspeople. Mercifully, the halftime whistle stopped the game. The score: Country Town 3, Jung-Wha 1.

At the intermission, all of us were cursing. Did we sail five hundred *li* of Yangtse River to be beaten by some country bumpkins? How could we, the Korean revolutionaries, allow such humiliation? We all swore we would do everything possible to absolve ourselves. When we returned to the field, our rising anger, mingled with the feeling of shame, only helped to raise further havoc; we were plainly outsmarted and outplayed. When the ball was passed to me, I tried to dribble it down the sideline, but the country player would anticipate all my moves and steal the ball. And when I chased and caught up with him, he showed tricks with his feet I had never seen before; he made me look foolish. And such was the case with every one of our players at every position. Now we all lost our tempers and our interest in the game as well. We only wanted to provoke a fight. This desperate tactic seemed to work and we scored a goal. But it was only a respite; they scored another goal immediately. The townspeople were delirious, which didn't ease our pain.

Following yet another goal by our opponents, we found the excuse we were looking for. Our fullback, the biggest man on our team, was knocked down in a shoving match. He jumped up, went after the "country-town" player, and knocked him down with his fist. Like lightning, a free-for-all erupted, and the townspeople converged on the field to join the melee. It was utter madness. By some miracle, every one of us managed to escape and retreat to the dormitory. With a quick change of clothes, and the bundles tucked under our arms, we safely ran out of the school. But we dared not pass through the town. Fortunately we found a peasants' inn on the outskirts and checked in for the night. We didn't have any supper that evening and we didn't sleep much. At dawn, before the town awoke, we sneaked our way to the harbor and got on the first boat heading for Nanking. The boat ride back was interminable; there was not much conversation and certainly no singing of revolutionary songs!

In time, the pangs of shame passed away and I finished my second year at Jung-Wha. I returned home to Shanghai for the summer vacation. Once again, all the Young Revolutionaries, now attending high schools in various parts of China, assembled in Shanghai. The death of the Chinese gangster had been forgotten and we were safe. Now our common concern was the quality of education we were receiving in the Chinese schools. The ever-present hunger and the unheated rooms in the winter were not as serious as the level of education; there was a total lack of any social or political studies. We talked in anguish and speculated on possible solutions. Some thought they could try to enter a university the following year while others confided their dreams to go to Russia for higher education. To the surprise of everyone I declared that, as for me, I would go to America for my education. This spurt of inspiration lingered in me like a seed, expanding and germinating into an obsession. I had to go to America. But how? Actually this new dream was not altogether unfounded. In early childhood, I had learned that I was born in Hawaii and somehow that made me an American citizen. So, I could travel freely to America if I could only afford the necessary expenses. Where and how could I find the money? Wrestling with the problem for days, I finally struck on a plan of action which would take me to America without too much delay.

To carry out the plan, I needed to have at least ten silver dollars—a small fortune. But finding such a large sum of money was indeed remote. Why not steal! The idea flashed through my head, and with fright I dismissed it promptly. But the idea would not disappear; it lingered on. It wouldn't be for just a selfish purpose . . . it was for an important and worthwhile cause . . . the money would be used to find a benefactor who would sponsor my trip to America. Besides, I would reimburse it many times over when I obtained the funds.

The picture of a jar filled with silver dollars appeared in my mind; it was Umma's money jar kept on the kitchen shelf. Oh, no! How could I steal Umma's precious money! I would be stealing from my whole family, depriving them of their daily necessities! Then, again, I excused myself: I would only be borrowing the money for a few days; it would be replaced very shortly. So, convincing and fortifying myself, I committed a most dastardly sin: I stole ten silver dollars out of Umma's money jar. I was so shaken with shame and fright, I ran out of the house without even leaving a note.

I went straight to the Whangpoo River docks and bought a one-way ticket to Ku-Lung, a thousand *li* north of Shanghai on the Yangtse River. I had to pay seven dollars one way, but I wasn't particularly worried about the return fare. This exhilarating boat trip was to be the first stage of a journey which would eventually lead to the sea voyage across the Pacific to America. At noon, the boat passed by Nanking, the home of Jung-Wha Middle Academy which held so many rich memories. Later, we passed the little riverport where we had disgraced ourselves at a soccer game. Our boat then entered the turbulent gorges of the Yangtse. The boat began to struggle against the angry waters and its forward movement slowed until it began to founder. How could our little boat possibly conquer the wild flow of the gorge?

Suddenly, I saw a boatman on the deck hurling a line onto the shore. A group of half-stripped workmen caught the line and hauled it until a heavy rope reached them. Now joined by other workmen, they slung the rope over their shoulders and began to pull. In unison, they leaned mightily and started a slow, torturous march. The boat began to move over the gorge, and as the rhythmic steps of the workmen quickened, it floated slowly over the churning waters. When at last we reached calm waters, a steam winch on the boat wound the rope back onto the deck and we were able to make speedier progress. Before arriving at our destination, however, we had to pass through a few more gorges and the painful human propulsion was repeated.

The sun had already set when we reached Ku-Lung. The docks were in semidarkness with only a few kerosene lanterns lighting the path for the passengers. I followed the crowd and stepped off the boat feeling glad to have completed the first stage of my grand plan. The next challenge was to find a way to scale the mountain which rose straight up from the river. At the top of the precipitous peak, I was told, was Ku-Lung, the famous resort where all the Americans spent the summer. Mr. Smith, my English teacher at Jung-Wha, had told me that's where he would be through the summer. And that was where the next step of my secret design would be accomplished: find Mr. Smith, borrow the money from him, and be on my way to America. But just now, I had to find a way to get to the top of that mountain, thousands of feet high. I noticed those who were also going to Ku-Lung going to the line of waiting sedan chairs and each climbing into a seat. I asked the sedan carriers how much it cost. "Two dollars," I was told. I paid and climbed onto a rather flimsy chair. Somewhat worried, I fingered the single dollar left in my pocket.

Two carriers, one in front and one in back, lifted the chair, put the two bamboo bars attached to the sides of the chair on their shoulders, and began the climb. I held onto the bouncing chair and peered into the dark outlines of the mountain. I could hardly discern the narrow path which spiraled up the face of the mountain. I dared not look down to see how in such black darkness the carriers knew where the path was; I only marveled at their steady rhythmic climb. For nearly an hour I was in the grip of mounting nervous tension, and at the height, where swirling clouds engulfed us, I was on the verge of a panic. Fortunately, as we negotiated the darkest corner, the bright moon rose over the peak and lit our way.

The caravan of sedan chairs finally crossed the last ridge and emerged onto a plateau, and what we beheld there was a veritable fairyland: it was Ku-Lung. The entire town, with paved streets, was lit with dazzling electric lights showing the tree-filled park in the center and a row of pretty houses along the circular rim of the park. Mr. Smith, my English teacher, had to be living in one of those houses. But which one? It was past midnight and the town was in deep sleep; how could I find the right house? The thought of spending the rest of the night in the park made me shiver and compelled me to walk up to the nearest house and knock on the door. No answer. I knocked again, louder and longer. I heard footsteps and then a voice, obviously an American.

"Who is it?"

"I am looking for Mr. Smith," I answered hopefully.

"Mr. Smith?"

"Yes, Mr. Smith from Jung-Wha Middle School in Nanking."

The door opened and, startled to see me standing there, an American mumbled something in rapid-fire English which I couldn't understand. Then, regaining his composure, he pointed at a house across the park.

"There," he pointed, "that house next to the big tree, that's Mr. Smith's house." Before I could thank him, he slammed the door and disappeared.

Ah, at last! A thousand *li* on the Yangtse River, a precarious sedan ride up the forbidding mountain, and now in Ku-Lung, standing before the very house which held the answer to my dream—I felt almost on my way to America. But at that moment, just when my grand design was about to be fulfilled, I was seized with sudden doubt. That was too painful. To reassure myself, I walked up to the house next to the big tree and knocked. A long wait. I knocked again and again. Finally I heard some stirring inside and then a voice.

"Who is it?" It was Mr. Smith.

"Peter Hyun from Jung-Wha!"

"Peter who?" Mr. Smith's voice seemed to quiver.

"Peter Hyun from Jung-Wha in Nanking," I answered as slowly

as possible. A long silence and then the door opened. Mr. Smith and I looked at each other in disbelief; no words from either of us. It was Mr. Smith who finally broke the awkward silence: "Come in, come in, come in from the cold. . . ."

After setting me down in a chair, he started to pace back and forth, shaking his head and mumbling to himself. With my meager English, I couldn't understand what he was saying except for a few words such as, "What in the world! . . . Heavens! . . . Oh, heavens! . . . Don't understand!" I heard him repeat "Heavens!" several times and "Oh, God!" again and again as though he was praying. He then groaned, "It's three o'clock! Three o'clock! Three in the morning!"

When he had calmed himself sufficiently, he came and sat beside me. "What's this midnight visit all about?" he asked haltingly. In my broken English, I explained the reason for my surprise appearance. I had made up my mind to get an education in America. I was born in Hawaii, so I could go there. Only in America would I get a good education. All I needed was one hundred American dollars—sixty for the steerage boat fare and the rest to tide me over until I found a school and a job. Mr. Smith shook his head again and began to rock himself in his chair, back and forth, back and forth. For a moment I was afraid he was becoming ill. Steadying himself finally, "Peter, my dear Peter," he pleaded, "I don't have one hundred dollars. I am not a rich man. I am only a poor missionary."

I didn't believe him. I restated my proposal. "Mr. Smith, only one hundred dollars. It will give me my education. . . . I'll pay you back . . . pay you back ten times one hundred when I finish my education."

Mr. Smith rose from his seat, came over, and patted me. "We must go to bed now," he said. "We will talk about it in the morning." He led me to a couch with some blankets, showed me where the bathroom was, and bid me good-night. So for the time being my plans were left suspended. Lying in an American bed, I tried to review the events since I left home with ten stolen silver dollars. My memory slowly faded and fatigue overwhelmed me.

In the morning, I met Mr. Smith's wife and their two young sons who gaped at me with open mouths. Mrs. Smith sent them away and invited me to the table for breakfast. Sitting there I couldn't help noticing the furtive glances of the two children crouched in the adjacent room. A Chinese servant bringing a platter of food saw me and stopped in his tracks. Mrs. Smith introduced me to the Chinese who kept smiling foolishly. This was my first experience at dining with Americans. The food looked exotic and appetizing, but I was too agitated to eat anything.

The breakfast over, Mr. Smith took me to the same room where we had met the night before. He handed me an envelope. "Peter, here is ten dollars. You can get a ticket on the boat and return to Shanghai. I will see you at Jung-Wha when the school opens." I don't remember exactly how I managed to come down from the mountain town. And on the long and lonely trip back to Shanghai, I consoled myself by thinking of all the benefits of my futile undertaking: two thousand *li* of Yangtse River sailing, watching a hundred men pull the boat over the gorges, and seeing Ku-Lung, the fairyland where the Americans kept cool in the summer. But most important of all, I learned that borrowing money, especially from an American, was not an easy matter.

Umma was beside herself when she saw me trudging home. Without leaving a clue, I had left home and been gone for three days. She hugged me and cried, which made me cry too. After supper, surrounded by all my brothers and sisters (Father was away as usual), I told them the sad and funny story of my adventure.

11

MISSION TO
AMERICA

IN MAY 1920, Father was appointed head of the Korean Commission in Washington, D.C. The commission, created by the Provisional Government in Shanghai, was charged with the responsibility of promoting and directing activities around the world to gain goodwill and support in Korea's struggle for independence. The official notice of Father's appointment, strangely, did not come from the government center in Shanghai but from the United States bearing the signature of Dr. Syngman Rhee. Why? The Provisional Government had elected Rhee to its cabinet and conferred on him the title of premier. But Rhee much preferred to be known as the president, and represented himself as such to all the Koreans living in America and Hawaii as well as in his dealings with American officials. Rhee refused to come to Shanghai and join the revolutionary leaders for fear of "the bad living conditions in China." So the head of the Provisional Government conducted his business alone in the United States thousands of miles away from its center and away from all of his associates.

Why was such a disjointed and unwieldy operation tolerated? Rhee had spent all of his adult life in security and comfort in America while his compatriots were waging a life and death struggle against the Japanese in Korea and Manchuria. Why then was Rhee named as head of the Provisional Government? It was an expedient political move. Despite historical experiences to the contrary, the revolutionary leaders still believed and hoped for American recognition and support for the Korean cause. By electing Rhee, the man who had lived in America for so many years, who was educated there, and who would be more familiar with the American political scene than anyone else, they had hoped he would play a decisive role in securing American aid. What they failed to take into account was Rhee's supreme ego, his driving personal ambition, and his uncompromising and ruthless method of dealing with all critics. They might have suspected such a character by the romanized spelling of his name: R-H-E-E. His name is among the most popular Korean surnames, including the name of the last Korean king, spelled phonetically L-E-E. But to distinguish his name from all other Koreans, he chose to spell it R-H-E-E: Dr. Syngman Rhee.

His image as a patriot emerged out of the historic period of struggle against the Japanese. It stemmed from his participation in the Independence Club, the first organized effort to repel the Japanese encroachment. It was organized in 1896 under the leadership of Dr. Phillip Jaisohn, a Korean emigrant to America who had become a doctor of medicine and then returned to Korea to rally its youth to combat the Japanese threat. Rhee, or Lee at the time, was one of the junior members of the Independence Club.

Under pressure from the Japanese, Dr. Jaisohn was forced to return to America, the club was smashed, and all its leaders, my grandfather among them, were arrested and imprisoned. Rhee was one of the prisoners, and upon his release he fled to the United States. An honorary Ph.D. degree was conferred by an American college and raised the image of Rhee as a great scholar as well as a patriot. While growing up in Seoul, I remember hearing the name of Dr. Syngman Rhee; it had a magical ring, and whenever his name was uttered, it cast a spellbinding sense of admiration and respect. With such a background of national adulation together with the almost mystical belief in American aid as the decisive factor in achieving Korean indepdendence, Rhee's election as the head of the Provisional Government was as natural as it was expedient.

Rhee's one notable accomplishment during his years in America was the organization of the Korean Dong Gee Whai—Society of Comrades. It was meant to be a center of patriotic Koreans living in the United States and Hawaii. In reality, it maintained no tie with the center of the independence movement in Shanghai and served only as an organ for the consolidation of Rhee's power and influence. It further served to strengthen Rhee's financial hold, for each member of the society was pledged to donate a part of his earnings to it. No one would ever know how much money had fallen into Rhee's coffers, for it was never accountable to anyone.

When the Korean Provisional Government was established in Shanghai, in 1920, groups of Koreans throughout the United States and Hawaii, in opposition to Rhee's Society of Comrades, formed the Korean National Association whose aim was to channel all moral and material support to the beleaguered center in Shanghai. Throughout the years when the revolutionaries in Shanghai were in desperate need of funds, from all the money he had collected from the Koreans, Rhee never shared a single dollar with his colleagues in Shanghai. And when he began representing himself as the president of Korea, Rhee's prestige rose and his fortune grew in direct proportion as well.

Rhee began issuing a "Korean National Bond" which the members of his society were obliged to purchase; the bonds were redeemable with interest upon the regaining of Korea's national independence. In later years, I had the chance to look at these "bonds" issued and sold by Rhee to the Korean immigrants. On the island of Kauai, I often accompanied Father on his visits to the Korean plantation laborers who proudly showed us the "National Bonds" they had bought. They had paid for them out of their dollar-a-day earnings and regarded them as their family treasure. They regarded the "bonds" as their passports with which one day, they dreamed, they would return to their homeland in the company of their president, Syngman Rhee. These dreams never materialized.

The leaders in Shanghai were becoming weary of Rhee's solitary role and growing impatient with his inaction on getting the long-awaited U.S. aid. Perhaps the appointment of Father as head of the Korean Commission and dispatching him to the United States was an expression of their dissatisfaction with Rhee, and an attempt to bypass him and make a direct appeal to the U.S. government through my father.

Unaware of the monolithic stronghold of Rhee's America, Father accepted his appointment, and on June 25, 1920, he embarked on his long journey to the United States. To avoid possible capture by the Japanese, instead of the direct route across the Pacific he boarded the French liner SS *Porthos* in Shanghai which would carry him through Southeast Asia, India, the Mediterranean, and finally across the Atlantic to New York. His odyssey consumed nearly two months, mostly on the seas. But for Father, the long voyage was neither tedious nor boring. He kept a meticulous diary of his journey, and from his journal I've read the highlights of the initial phase of his mission to America.

Aboard the ship, he spent the first days seeking out other Asian passengers. He was surprised to discover many young Chinese students bound for schools in Europe. He conceived and organized a Chinese Student League and held daily meetings for cultural and political discussions. At the stopovers in Hong Kong and Saigon, Father contacted the Chinese student organizations there and established formal affiliations for his "Sailing Student League."

In Saigon there was a five-day layover, and Father went ashore and spent much time touring the city. He was impressed with the wide boulevards and sidewalks lined with lush tropical trees. The buildings, he noted, were of French architecture, and most of the businesses were owned and managed by the French. Only the little tobacco shops were owned and run by Chinese and Hindus. He felt rather uncomfortable to see so many French soldiers and sailors in the city and for the boat to be escorted out of the harbor by a fleet of French airplanes.

After a stopover in Singapore, the ship passed through the Straits of Malacca and entered the Indian Ocean. Father spent the long days and nights reading or discussing and debating with the students. The ship reached the port city of Colombo on the Indian island of Ceylon. When Father, together with three other Asian passengers, wanted to go ashore, a Hindu policeman barred the way. But Father quickly found the practice of bribery to be quite universal; pressing a sum of money into the palm of the policeman immediately transformed them into welcome visitors. Father wrote in his diary, "In Colombo, found an Arabian hotel where my friends and I experienced a most memorable lunch."

The ship passed little Laccadive Island as Father was reading *Korea's Fight for Freedom* by F. A. McKenzie. As they approached the African coast, they were met by a stormy sea. The ship waged a mighty struggle as she slowly passed the island of Socotra, controlled by the British, and, the next day, the little port of Djibouti, controlled by the French.

The ship was now sailing through the Red Sea. Father could see Arabia on one side and Africa on the other. The weather then changed; the sea became calm and the temperature rose ever higher. That was when a fierce fight broke out aboard ship between an Arabian and an Algerian student. It was violent and fearful, and the men had to be subdued and put in the ship's prison. This outbreak of violence between two Arab students greatly disturbed Father, and he spent much of the night walking the deck, watching the pink and blue sky, and meditating. On the morning of July 28, he rose at 4:00 A.M., as was his habit, and immediately washed his face, as was the Korean custom. He then sat down and composed a poem in the classical Chinese form. Its free translation:

> Open your eyes toward the sea,
> And face the fierce wind.
> Somewhere spring flowers are smiling,
> And elsewhere autumn leaves are falling.
> Cannot men find the design
> To bring Peace everywhere?

The SS *Porthos* was now approaching the Suez Canal. It stopped at the port to unload the cargo and then moved through the long canal. It took more than twenty-four hours to complete the crossing and finally arrive at Port Said. Father and his friends went ashore and, feeling like pilgrims, set their feet on the land of Egypt—the land of Pharaohs, Jews, and Moses. Father wished to taste Egyptian food; he bought the most exotic he could find and took it aboard to share with his students.

The next day, the ship began its journey on the Mediterranean Sea. Among the many islands they passed, Father was deeply moved at the sight of the island of Crete; that was where, Father mused, St. Paul had traveled and preached. They also passed the island of Corsica where Napoleon Bonaparte was born.

The ship arrived at Marseilles on August 4—forty days after departure from Shanghai. Father held a final meeting with the Chinese students and urged them to return home and help their country when they finished their education. Eager to reach the schools, the students immediately left for Paris by train. Father spent several days around Marseilles to take in the sights of yet another new country before boarding the train for Paris. He was met by a few Koreans living in Paris with whose help he unraveled the complex puzzle dealing with his passport and visas. Father was a Korean, but he was traveling with a Chinese passport issued in Shanghai. All this had to be verified, first at the Chinese consulate in order to obtain a Chinese visa to go to the United States. All the documents then had to be examined and approved by the U.S. consulate in order to obtain an American visa. When all this was satisfactorily completed, once again the documents had to be scrutinized and approved; this time, by the French authorities. Father had spent ten days at the embassies and consulates, and finally, on August 14, he got on the French liner SS *Lafayette* and sailed out of Le Havre. He was heading for the final destination of his mission to America.

The journey crossing the Atlantic was rather uneventful. Most of the passengers were Americans and Europeans who weren't much interested in politics. But Father did become acquainted with two American missionaries returning home on furlough; one was from Boston and the other from somewhere in Arkansas. Father's diary also mentions meeting a Chinese YMCA worker with whom he enjoyed the daily exercises in the ship's gym. He was glad to have the free hours which he used to read and study the text of St. Matthew. The SS *Lafayette* docked in New York harbor on August 23—the fifty-ninth day since his embarkation in Shanghai. Two Korean representatives met him and escorted him to the Grand Hotel. His visit in New York was to be only a courtesy call to meet some of the Korean community leaders. They were all elated to meet one of the organizers of the March First uprising who was now a member of the Provisional Government. Father's arrival in New York marked the first appearance of a Korean revolutionary leader coming directly from the center of their struggle—Shanghai. He was swamped with questions: What is the state of affairs in Shanghai, how is the health of their leaders, what are the latest developments inside Korea? Father was glad to meet and talk to them, but his mind was fixed on Washington, D.C., his ultimate destination.

To forestall further delay, he left the next day for Washington, and there he went directly to the Korean Commission office. Father was to meet its chairman, Dr. Kim Kiu-Sik, whom he was replacing. They had been anxiously waiting for him and were not a little concerned about his long-delayed arrival. A suitable lodging had been secured for Father at the home of a Mr. and Mrs. King. He was briefed on the activities of the Korean Commission in America and Europe, and was informed of all of its responsibilities. Among the documents, Father noted the monthly budget of the commission's centers:

Washington, D.C.	$1,500
Philadelphia	$800
Paris	$500
Others	$1,200
Total	$4,000

Father's plan of action was to organize and rally all the Koreans living in the United States, Mexico, and Cuba to support the work of the Korean Commission. He launched the campaign by touring and visiting all the little Korean communities scattered around the country. His initial drive was concentrated on the West Coast: San Francisco and Los Angeles primarily, but not neglecting smaller towns wherever a few Koreans lived. He was deeply moved to find his compatriots in such little California towns as Delano, Modesto, Riverside, Maxwell, and Merced. The next important area was the Pacific Northwest, and he toured through Oregon and Washington. He completed the full circle by visiting Detroit and Chicago. These travels and visits to the scattered Korean communities reminded him of his work in the Hawaiian Islands as a traveling preacher when he was building Christian churches. Now he was traveling through the United States building the Korean independence movement.

Just as the sugar plantation laborers had supported his missionary work in Hawaii, the Korean immigrants throughout the United States now rallied around his political work. Money began to pour in and Father began to expand the activities of the commission.

Not a little of his success, it might be observed, could be attributed to a fortunate coincidence: the absence of Syngman Rhee in the United States at the time. There was no opposition or obstacle to

Father's undertakings. After a prolonged refusal to join his colleagues, Rhee had finally decided to go to Shanghai just as Father reached the American shores. What prompted him to leave the rich and profitable stamping ground of America was his overriding desire to have his title as president officially conferred by the Provisional Government in Shanghai. Undoubtedly, Rhee received reports of Father's successful activities in the United States which must have irked him considerably, but he was helpless to halt the rise of a rival who might challenge his power and influence in America.

In February 1921, Father made a startling discovery. In the files of the Korean Commission he found an official document of the Korean Provisional Government: his appointment as ambassador plenipotentiary to the United States of America. Why had this never been delivered to him? Who hid such an important document and why? He was unable to fathom the reasons until many months later when other strange events took place. At the moment, he was elated with his new position as Korea's ambassador, for now, using his authority, he could take Korea's case to the highest level of American government.

Father moved quickly to open an official headquarters of the Provisional Government in Washington, D.C. From Shanghai, Rhee objected to the move but he was overruled. In April 1921, the Korean Legation was established at 1325 Massachusetts Avenue N.W., Washington, D.C., and the formal announcement of its opening was sent to all the diplomatic representatives and to the members of Congress. Father then formally presented his credentials to the U.S. government. He retained a Mr. Finkle and G. W. Stern as legal and political advisors respectively. With their help, he drafted a petition for U.S. recognition and on May 11, 1921, Father presented it to the secretary of state, Charles Evans Hughes.

Father's work in the United States was receiving growing support and wide international attention. It was beyond Syngman Rhee's nature or temperament to tolerate such accolades for anyone other than himself, especially in America, which he considered his own personal territory. Even then, in the early twenties, Rhee had developed a strong-arm method of dealing with his rivals. It was discovered later that in the centers of his organization throughout the United States and Hawaii, he had maintained bands of "enforcers." The use of force to foster his personal power eventually spelled Rhee's doom, however.

When in 1948, under the aegis of the American Occupation Army and the United Nations, Syngman Rhee became president of the Republic of Korea (South Korea), he freely applied his strong-arm tactics as national policy. It was a policy to suppress all semblance of criticism or opposition. To the consternation of the United States who continued to maintain its occupation army and pour hundreds of millions of dollars into South Korea annually, and to the consternation of the United Nations who had certified Rhee's election in South Korea as constituting "a valid expression of the free will of the electorate," Syngman Rhee's regime grew into a dictatorship. It was inevitable that his rule would topple as it did in 1960 when the students spearheaded a revolt against him.

Father first tasted Rhee's wrath in 1921 in Washington, D.C., but he did not anticipate that Rhee's drive for power would override all other considerations, including the national interest directed by the Provisional Government. In June 1921, Father wrote in his journal: "On a certain morning in June 1921, I went to my office at the Korean Commission to find myself unable to enter. I could not open the entrance door with my key because someone had changed the lock on the door. I went immediately to the bank. I discovered that my name was no longer valid in all the official bank accounts. They had been transferred to the name of Phillip Jaisohn." Jaisohn's Korean name was So Chae-P'il; he had led the early student revolt in 1896. Father then wrote, "There were no instructions from Shanghai, either from the Provisional Government or Syngman Rhee. But I knew that the plot against me made it impossible for me to carry on. I had no choice but to return to Shanghai."

Father suspected that only Syngman Rhee would resort to such dastardly means of stopping his work in the United States. With what funds he had on hand, Father traveled to San Francisco and from there to Hawaii, where he held many a happy reunion with the Koreans he had helped to settle in the sugar plantations. He also visited with Dr. Wadman of his early days of mission work and with Dr. Fry, the new superintendent of the Hawaiian Methodist Church. Learning of the disgraceful encounter in Washington and Father's predicament, his supporters in Hawaii raised $700 for his return passage to China.

He arrived in Shanghai in time to face the bleakest year of the Korean independence movement. The financial situation of the movement had so deteriorated and the mere day-to-day struggle to survive had become so great that Father's attempt to resolve his Washington experience became insignificant by comparison. Besides, Rhee had returned to the United States, there to direct his own independence movement as he wished without the bother of the Provisional Government. Soon after his return to China, Father was called to undertake yet another mission, and despite his recent disillusionment, he accepted.

It was a mission to Moscow: an attempt to salvage the faltering movement by seeking aid from the Soviets. The Korean revolutionaries in Shanghai had been extended an invitation by the Soviet government to attend the Second Internationale in Moscow. It was a historic conclave for the defense of the newborn Union of Soviet Socialist Republics and for all colonial peoples throughout the world whose aspirations for national freedom were emerging everywhere. Father's mission as a Korean delegate was to plead his country's cause in Moscow for whatever aid the Soviets had to offer, and before the world assembly of the colonial peoples for their pledge of solidarity with the Koreans.

Once again Father traversed Manchuria, dodging the Japanese police and eluding spies, and reached Vladivostok where he boarded the Trans-Siberian railway. It was a slow and precarious ride, for much of the railroad had been damaged through sabotage by the retreating "White Guard" Czarist army and by the "Allies" including the U.S. Expeditionary Force who fought the Bolsheviks in a determined effort to overthrow the new Soviet government. The battered old train took nearly a month to travel across the war-devastated Russian continent— a whole month to haul the revolutionaries from all over Asia to the revolutionary capital of Moscow.

Throughout the long ride, Father had ample time to meet other peoples and learn how they waged their struggle for independence and freedom. In all the exchanges of experiences and ideas, however, he was made to feel a grave handicap: he was a Christian minister. He was the exception among the passengers, all of whom represented workers' and peasants' organizations. Some did not hide their scorn of Father as a merchant of religion, the "opiate of the people." But as time passed, something happened which elevated his status among the proletariat and gained him much respect.

Suddenly Father became "Comrade Hyun"! What he did on the train was what he had done all his life. A habitual early riser, he was the first to wake up in the morning. After his morning ritual, he would find a broom and start sweeping the train, not only his own car but the whole train. An entry in his journal: "None of the proletariat would do any work, so I, the 'merchant of opiates,' worked and kept the train clean." This was how Father became the respected "comrade" of all his fellow passengers.

Father described the pitiful devastation of the country and the painful sight of people suffering with hunger. Thousands were dying of starvation every day. "Do you know what we ate for a month on the train?" Father asked as he told us the story of his long train ride. "Black bread and water," he said, "and I had to spit out bits of straw and stone before I could swallow."

I didn't know what the "Second Internationale" was about, and Father's journal failed to elucidate. However, he does mention an important session of all the colonial delegates with the leader of the Russian revolution, Vladimir Ilyich Lenin. Of his impression of Lenin, Father wrote: "He was a great man with an enormous head which must have been filled with knowledge and wisdom. He was very kind and understanding. He listened to every delegate, including me, with all his attention. I was introduced to Lenin as a 'Comrade Minister.' "

Father met with other Russian leaders and discussed the Korean independence movement and its desperate need for help. Among others, he met and exchanged views with Leon Trotsky, then the commissar of the Red Army. At the close of the conclave, the delegates scattered over the world, encouraged, if not by the prospect of immediate material aid, then at least with mutual recognition of the immensity of their common struggle. There was also an affirmation of their determination to carry on the struggle in their homeland upon their return. Shanghai was Father's home in exile. He returned there and submitted his report of the mission to Moscow. He then faced the harshest year of his life; the year was 1923.

Father refused to beg. He believed in his own "faith to overcome all worldly hardships." Meanwhile, his family was reduced to living on a daily bowl of noodles for each member. One day, after his morning prayer, Father noticed an advertisement in the *China Press,* a Shanghai

English newspaper. "Salesman wanted," it said. It had been placed by an English drug company. Father found the DeWitt Drug Company and applied for the job.

"What's your experience?" he was asked.

"I worked for the Korean independence movement," Father replied.

"That's all right," the manager said, who happened to be an Irishman. "But can you speak Chinese?"

"Yes, some," Father said, and added, "I would like to start working right away."

The manager agreed and handed him a bundle of posters and a salesman's grip with brief instructions. Father immediately went out on the streets of Shanghai and began his work. Early in the afternoon, Father returned to the office and reported the results; all the posters had been distributed and he brought back several hundred dollars' worth of orders for the patent medicine. The manager, pleased with Father's initial work, offered to pay him a hundred dollars per month plus travel expenses if he would agree to work in Manchuria.

It was a way to save his family from starvation. Once more, Father sailed out of Shanghai and headed for the plains of Manchuria. Trudging through towns large and small, he covered the walls with the posters and sold the English patent medicine to everyone who could afford it. His travels as a salesman led him to the city of Mukden. There he was overpowered by his memories. It was in this strange city a scant four years ago that he began his career as a revolutionary. This was where he first met Chai Chang-Sik and other Korean expatriates. It was in this same city that he had summoned the reporters of the Western press and released the news of the Korean uprising. After plodding around the world for that cause ever since, he was now back in the same city. Only now he was walking the streets of Mukden with an armful of posters and a bag of patent medicine to keep his body and soul together, and to save poor Umma and his eight children from starvation.

12

THE CRISIS

For four years, the struggle for Korean independence was carried on by a handful of patriots. From the little center in Shanghai, their activities reached vital areas all around the world. With pamphlets, pictures, and sometimes with emissaries, the appeals for help were sent out to London, Paris, Moscow, Nanking, and Washington. Among other numerous activities, the most courageous were the guerrilla warfare against the Japanese in Manchuria and the underground movement inside Korea. The underground was the lifeline sustaining not only the morale of the people but also the financial aid to the Provisional Government in Shanghai.

Of course, the struggle exacted a heavy toll in human suffering. The number of farmers tortured and killed, the number of women raped and dismembered, and the number of students who disappeared will never be known. Under the relentless Japanese drive, slowly but surely, the whole fabric of the movement was being ripped apart. The task of maintaining contact with local centers grew increasingly difficult.

From the beginning, the hope of eventual success was based on support and aid from the United States. At the time, it didn't seem to be such an empty dream. After all, wasn't the March First uprising born out of President Wilson's declaration regarding "the right of all nations for self-determination"? Wasn't there a treaty of mutual aid between the United States and Korea? Was it a mistake for millions of Koreans to have embraced the religion preached by the American missionaries? Was it foolish to have believed in the new faith and to have placed so much trust in its homeland America—"The Land of Freedom"?

But repeated appeals for help were ignored by America. The U.S. policy on colonial nations was not only devastating to the Korean independence movement, but also damaging to the aspirations of all colonial peoples. Out of World War I, the United States had emerged as the richest and the most powerful nation; America became the world's trader, lender, and overseer. At the same time, America carved an image of itself as the world's liberator. Japan, in the meanwhile, thrust ahead as the new rising power in Asia. Certainly, it was far more profitable for the United States to bind closer ties with the growing industrial and military power, Japan, than to jeopardize national interests by rendering any aid to the weakling, Korea. The U.S. "Korea policy" was a tacit approval of Japan's conquest; Japan was given a free hand to deal with Korea in any way it chose.

Koreans, by the hundreds, disappeared overnight while others were imprisoned and tortured. Villages were surrounded by Japanese troops and police, the populace massacred, homes burned to the ground. Young boys and girls sacrificed their lives in vain attempts to keep the independence movement alive. But under the intensifying reign of terror, the underground inevitably collapsed, and with it the lifeline of the movement: the flow of money for its center in Shanghai.

For the Provisional Government, it was now a question of survival. First, they gave up their office building. Next, they trimmed the expenses of the officials to the absolute minimum. It was at this time of despair that I heard the story of a young patriot who brought a sackful of money to the beleaguered leaders one day but refused to divulge its source. Only months later, when the fear of a police raid had died down, the full story came to light.

Late one night, the youth and a comrade drove a rented automobile to Tse-Ma-Loo—the "Four Horse Street." Located in the center of the city, the street was notorious for the concentration of whorehouses and gambling dens. They stopped in front of a large, plush casino. The driver remained in the car while the young revolutionary entered the building. Posing as a drunken gambler, he managed to pass through the guarded gates to the main gambling room.

There he whipped out an automatic and threatened to shoot anyone who moved. He flung a canvas bag on the table and ordered the manager to collect all the money and fill it. With so many silver dollars, the bag might have weighed a ton, but he picked it up and slung it over his shoulder. His gun trained on the bewildered gamblers, he stepped backwards toward the door. He shouted his final warning—anyone trying to open the door after him would be shot. He stepped out and locked the door. His comrade saw him emerging from the casino and leaped out of the car, pushed his friend with the heavy load into it, and drove off.

Sometime later, I met this astonishing bandit. He was so slight and fragile I couldn't believe he'd really stolen a bagful of money from the casino. Of course, the money was put to immediate use. But eventually, just as Father had done, most of the leaders and cadres had to scatter and go wherever they could find a livelihood. The exception was Syngman Rhee, who had an easy way out; he returned to America where his self-proclaimed title—president of the Provisional Government—gained him greater power and personal wealth. The members of his Dong Gee Whai faithfully made their monthly contributions for the "Independence Movement," none of which Rhee ever shared with his close-to-starving colleagues in Shanghai.

Defying the mounting hardships, a small group remained in Shanghai. Among them two heroes stand out in my mind: Kim Koo and Lyuh Woon Hyung. Kim Koo began his revolutionary career as a sergeant-at-arms in the first Korean Parliament. He organized a group of young revolutionaries as armed guards and provided security in the government center. In 1923, when all the leaders were forced to leave the center in search of a livelihood, Kim Koo clung to his post and eventually assumed the role of head of the Provisional Government.

By then Father had already returned to Hawaii to resume his religious work, but his heart had never really left Shanghai. Along with his new church work, he organized the Koreans in Hawaii to rally around Kim Koo and support the government. In his travels through many parts of the islands, Father never failed to take up a special collection and send the money each month to Kim Koo in Shanghai.

In 1929, encouraged by its growing economic ties with the Western powers and emboldened by its entrenchment in Korea, Japan launched its centuries-old dream: the conquest of China. The initial signal was the bombing of Shanghai. It was not so much an attack on China, but a test of the disposition of the Western powers. There was no protest, no retaliation. Japan marched in and took over Manchuria without firing a shot. The last Manchu emperor, Henry P'u Yi, was installed as the figurehead ruler of Manchuria, now renamed Manchukuo. It was the first step in the "Pan-Asian" plan—a plan to conquer all Asia and become the sole ruler.

The occupation of Manchuria secured, step by step, Japan advanced across the Chinese landmass. The infamous "Rape of Nanking" by the advancing Japanese force was only part of the ruthless design to conquer at all cost. Throughout these perilous times, Kim Koo was there in Shanghai, rallying young Koreans and waging guerrilla warfare against the Japanese with whatever available means. He offered Korean volunteers for China's defense, and Chiang Kai-shek gladly accepted his offer. A Korean brigade was organized and trained under Kim Koo, and then joined the Chinese Nationalist army at the front.

I was then in New York, where I helped to organize the "United Koreans to Aid China." We got a city permit and conducted a "Tag Day for China" on the streets of New York. With money collected from the American public, we bought a Studebaker ambulance and sent it to the Korean brigade in China. But that is far ahead of my story.

Lyuh Woon Hyung was a great leader as well, but quite different from Kim Koo. He was younger and handsome, and I cherished a secret envy of his dark bushy moustache. He was a friend of us young people. Among all the leaders, Lyuh was the only one who took time to come to the park and watch us play and talk to us. He would shout and cheer when we played soccer, and when one of us scored a goal, he would leap and clap like a boy. During the intermission, he'd join us and participate in planning our strategy. We forgot that he was one of the big leaders; he was one of us, he was our friend.

When the movement in Shanghai began to falter, Lyuh decided to return to Korea even though he faced probable arrest and imprisonment. He believed he could serve his country better among his own people. He was indeed arrested and imprisoned but somehow survived. When finally released, he resumed his work, but in an entirely different way. He spent his time with the young people, and through their athletic activities he taught them how to play, how to learn, and how to organize.

Toward the end of World War II, when the Japanese forces began to totter, Lyuh played a key role in establishing the Korean People's Republic and, under it, the People's Committees as governing bodies throughout the country. Before the arrival of the U.S. occupation army in September 1945, the Korean People's Committees disarmed the Japanese gendarmes and maintained peace and order. The People's Republic was functioning as a government throughout Korea, North and South. Its local committees were carrying out all the urgent tasks such as distribution of food and medicine, and even began to implement land reform.

Japan's defeat in World War II released the long-suppressed creative forces of the Korean people and generated a renaissance of art and culture. A "United Korean Cultural Reconstruction Society" was formed to promote various activities. They were carried out through the departments of literature, painting, music, dance, and theatre. Similar organizations were also being initiated in education, agriculture, and industry. It was at this time that Lyuh, on behalf of the People's Republic, sent an official message to Father. The message was: Father had been elected to the cabinet in absentia. Lyuh urged Father to accept and return to Korea. In declining the honor, Father wrote to Lyuh and said that he could not return as long as Korea remained divided into North and South.

So Korea was actually under self-rule long before Gen. John R. Hodge and the U.S. Seventh Army landed in South Korea and promulgated the "American Military Government" in September of 1945. One of the first acts of the AMG was to order the dissolution of the Korean People's Republic as well as all the local People's Committees. Next the AMG outlawed the Korean Communist Party and all "radical" organizations, including the Cultural Reconstruction Society. The AMG then invalidated all land reform under which the land confiscated from the rich had been distributed to the landless peasants.

In their place, the AMG proclaimed a policy of "free enterprise" under which the land was returned to the rich landlords, and the distribution of sorely needed food and medicine was transferred from the

People's Committees to the revived Korean Chamber of Commerce. The AMG also resurrected Korea's old monopolies, the textile and mining industries among them. The political climate was now ripe to bring Dr. Syngman Rhee from the United States and install him as president of the Republic of Korea (South Korea). To ensure Rhee's position and power, all opposition was systematically removed. The two great patriots, Kim Koo and Lyuh Woon Hyung, were conveniently eliminated by assassination in 1946–1947. But again, I am running ahead of my story.

Another victim of the demise in Shanghai was our Young Revolutionary Society. Having to give up all athletic and theatrical activities was sad enough, but the greater tragedy was the shattering of our dreams for a higher education. We became lost children. There were only two courses open for our salvation. One was to join the Korean guerrillas in Manchuria and fight the Japanese. I met and talked to some of them. They convinced me that to survive in the Manchurian underground, I had to be completely dedicated. The adventurous life of a guerrilla appealed to me. Some of them came to Shanghai periodically to obtain arms and money. One day, I was at a friend's house when a man brought in a large wooden box. The guerrilla fighters pried it open and let out a yell of excitement. The box was filled with guns and ammunition. Watching their enthusiasm and eagerness, I could hardly resist the temptation to join them.

The only other alternative for the young Korean revolutionaries was to follow the leadership of Park Huen-Young, the long-time friend of our family, the silent one. Somehow, Park had established contact with the new political movement of China: the Chinese Communist Party. Led by the son of a peasant, the movement was gaining a great following, especailly among the disenfranchised and landless peasants. The swelling wave of the movement reached Shanghai and began making inroads among the industrial laborers. For the first time in China's history, the working people were organizing into labor unions and were pressing demands for better pay and working conditions.

It was at this stage that Park established his contact with the Chinese Communist Party and received encouragement and aid. He had arrived at the belief that the only hope for achieving Korean independence was through alliance with the Communist movement. With their help, Park founded a school for young Korean revolutionaries. They not only studied the new theories of revolution but also engaged in practical activities of agitation and propaganda. The Koreans' major contribution was in assisting the Chinese Communists to organize factory workers into labor unions. It was a daring and dangerous activity, for the Chinese Nationalist government under Generalissimo Chiang Kai-shek was determined to stamp out the movement at all cost. Being arrested by the Shanghai police and turned over to Chiang meant certain death.

But in those days in Shanghai, the threat of death was no deterrent, especially for revolutionaries. It mattered little that anyone arrested disappeared or had their heads chopped off in public. It almost happened to me. Out of my friendship and admiration for Park's dedicated work for Korean independence, I had offered my services for whatever use he might have. He thanked me and promised he would call me whenever I was needed. He kept his promise.

Early one Sunday morning, following his instructions, I picked up a bundle of printed leaflets and went to the assigned area to distribute them. The leaflets, urging the people to attend a mass meeting, were issued in the name of the Communist Party of China, and anyone caught possessing or distributing them faced immediate arrest and an unknown fate.

I went from house to house slipping the leaflets under the gates, and at the stores I pushed them through whatever opening I could find. My instructions were to distribute them as quickly as possible before the people awoke and came out on the streets. In the midst of my hurried work, I suddenly caught sight of a dreaded figure coming toward me: a French policeman in his dark blue uniform, a short black cape, and a military hat. He held a wooden club in one hand and in the other he gripped a leash being pulled by a huge police dog.

I made an instant about-face and began walking away in the opposite direction. Barely controlling the urge to run, I moved faster and faster. Behind me, I could feel the policeman increasing his pace also. I turned a corner and dashed toward the French park, hoping the trees and the shrubbery would afford me some hiding place. As I began to run, I could hear the pounding footsteps of the policeman and the angry barking of the dog. I was terrified.

A short distance away, I saw a little brick building with the "W.C." sign. I tossed the bundle of leaflets behind a hedge, ran into the W.C., and bolted the flimsy lock inside. The dog's barking grew louder and more ferocious until it was just outside of where I was hiding. Mercifully, the dog's ear-splitting barks and the angry shouts of the policeman indicated that they were running around and around the hedge where I had thrown away the leaflets. I held my breath. Then, by a miracle, the dog and the policeman ran off and the barking faded. I came out trembling and managed to muster enough strength to run out of the park.

Back at the headquarters, I reported what had happened to Teacher Park. I was mortified by my failure and apologized. Teacher Park patted me.

"You were brave, Peter. You behaved well under fire."

" But I lost all the leaflets," I said.

"Remember, Peter," he consoled me, "your life is more valuable than the leaflets."

Sometime later, Teacher Park asked me to come to his headquarters. When I arrived there, I found three other young Korean revolutionaries waiting; I knew them by sight. Without any ceremony, Teacher Park handed out a piece of thin paper to each of us saying, "This is your passport to enter the Soviet Union at Vladivostok. Once there, you will be the guests of the Soviet government and travel on the Trans-Siberian railway to Moscow." The four of us were stunned. I couldn't believe I was one of the four chosen to be so honored. In a solemn voice, Teacher Park continued.

"You will travel separately taking different routes so that you will not be prey to the Japanese together. You will assemble in Vladivostok and board the train to Moscow." Listening to the terse travel plan, we could hardly hide our elation.

"Now," Teacher Park sounded ominous, "should any one of you be captured by the Japanese, you must immediately roll up the passport and swallow it." Only then did I understand why the passports, written in three languages, were printed on onionskin paper. At that moment, I felt humble and frightened. But in light of the events which soon followed, it became evident that my education and my destiny were not to be shaped in Russia.

One day shortly after this meeting, I returned home to be summoned by Umma.

"Pedro-ya!" Unmistakably, the tone of her voice signaled serious business.

"Yes, Umma," I answered and approached her gingerly.

"What is this, Pedro-ya?" To my amazement, she was waving the Russian passport in my face. I was sure I had carefully hidden it. How did she find it?

"Oh, it's nothing, Umma." I tried to appear carefree and unconcerned.

"Yes, it is something." Umma refused to be fooled. "You were planning to run away to Russia, weren't you?" I should have known better than to try to deceive my mother.

"Well," I said weakly, "that's the only place where I can get an education."

"No, it's not," she said, and without another word, she struck a match and put it to my precious passport. With a puff of smoke, my whole future seemed to disappear.

"Umma! Oh, Umma!" I cried. "Why did you do that?"

"Because," she said calmly, "you are not going to Russia where people are dying of starvation."

"Then where can I get an education?" I moaned.

"In America." Umma said it so casually that, for a moment, I believed her.

"But how? When?" It was all so hopeless.

"Someday," Umma intoned. "Somehow. . . ."

For days afterwards I was in limbo. I could not forgive Umma for burning my passport. Fortunately, a few weeks later, a great family event lifted me out of my depression: my dear Sister Alice was getting married. This was the first wedding in the Korean colony in Shanghai. The whole community was in a state of excitement, and everyone wanted to participate by doing something: sewing, decorating, cooking, or running errands. Even though the wedding would not be in the traditional Korean manner, Umma was determined to make it as Korean as she possibly could.

The groom was a stranger to us. The year before, determined to have Sister Alice obtain a modern education, Umma had hoarded enough money to send her to a school in Japan in secret. While in school she met Chung, a university graduate. From a first casual meeting, they became close friends and soon fell in love. So, Sister Alice brought Chung to Shanghai to have him meet the family and plan the wedding. Chung, I found, was handsome and pleasant enough, but secretly I had hoped to have Teacher Park as my brother-in-law.

The most important part of a Korean wedding is the feast, and for days Umma supervised its preparation. She worked with a group of ladies day and night concocting all the necessary dishes. At a respectable Korean wedding feast, there must be at least six kinds of meat, six kinds of fish, six kinds of poultry, and six kinds of salad, not to mention six kinds of rice and, of course, six kinds of *kim-chee*.

For my part, I was determined to do something special to please and honor my dear sister. The inspiration came to me early in the morning of the wedding day. The ceremony was to be in the Korean church at noon; I had barely enough time. I dressed hastily, and without waiting for breakfast, ran out of the house. I took the trolley and went to the center of the city where I found a beauty parlor. With all the "man of the world" manners I could muster, I told the lady that I wished to have wavy hair.

"It will cost five dollars," she said.

"Don't worry," I said, "I've got the money."

The lady set me in a chair and went to work. I shut my eyes and imagined I would soon look like an American movie star. Oh, how I would surprise everyone at the wedding! She poured some strong-smelling liquid over my hair, then washed and steamed, and finally twisted it around strange gadgets all over my head. I was then led to another chair where a huge crown was placed over my head. I was on fire and I had to endure it for a long while. What price beauty!

At last, the woman took the furnace off my head and removed all the gadgets. Smiling proudly, she held a mirror before me. At the sight, I almost fell out of my seat. The image in the mirror shocked me. After taking a deep breath, I opened my eyes for another look. It was indescribable. Instead of the soft wavy hair I had envisioned, my head was a round ball of tight curls. I asked the woman if she could take the curls out.

"Impossible," she said. And it was already nearing noon; I had to be back at home. I had to take several deep breaths before going into the house. Hiding my shame, I swaggered in nonchalantly. The first ones who saw me gasped and then began to giggle.

"Look! Look! Look at Peter!" Everyone turned, and their laughter grew into roars and shrieks.

"What did you do?" Umma saw me and moaned, "What did you do, Pedro-ya!"

"I wanted to look special for sister's wedding," I tried to explain. My eyes caught the sight of my brothers and sisters. Paul, the oldest one, just stared into space to avoid looking at me. Brother Joshua broke into a spasm of coughing while trying to stifle his laughing. Brother David was serious when he asked, "How did they make your hair look like that?" Sister Elizabeth was too embarrassed; she just hung her head and stared at the floor. Only my dear invalid sister Soon-Ok motioned to me and whispered, "It's all right, Pedro-ya. It's all right."

After the wedding ceremony, the feast took place at the house and was a great success. The guests were overwhelmed. They couldn't believe Umma had created all the traditional Korean dishes; it was a splendid feast commemorating an unforgettable event. When the celebration finally ended, suddenly I was seized with an overpowering sadness. In fact, I had to leave the house. My dearest sister! I had lost my dearest sister! Her name was now Chung, and she would go away to live with her husband in Korea. She was more than a sister; she was my friend, my guardian, my mentor. She knew all my secrets, my ambitions, my dreams. She was my counselor; she dispelled all my doubts and fears, encouraged and supported me in all my endeavors. And now she was gone.

13

DISCOVERY

ANOTHER EVENT during these tumultuous times carved a new milestone in my life. In the beginning, it was quite innocuous. A young Korean man appeared in Shanghai and was introduced to our family; his name was Chai. His credentials were that he knew Sister Alice's husband, Chung, and that he had graduated from college in Japan. He was accepted by everyone in the family. The only criticism was that he came from a very rich ramily and had a reputation of being a playboy. He was tall and slim and his good looks were marred only by a perpetual grin whenever he talked. It didn't take long before he began showing interest in Sister Elizabeth, but his courting was rather feeble, and no one, including my sister, took him seriously.

One day, grinning, he approached and addressed me in the respectful form even though I was almost ten years younger than he. "Pedro-Si," he asked, "how would you like to go to Soochow with me?" It was so sudden, I didn't know what to say.

"Pedro-Si," he grinned as he tried to explain, "I want to visit the famous city of Soochow, but I don't speak Chinese, and that's why I would like you to come with me."

"I don't know," I said. "I'll have to ask my mother." To my surprise, Umma consented readily, and one morning Chai and I got on the train to Soochow.

We arrived there at noon, and at my instructions to take us to a good hotel, the rickshawman dropped us off at an impressive place. I had never been inside such a luxurious hotel; the immense lobby was filled with carved tables and chairs. Varicolored silk shades with tassels adorned the porcelain lamps, and thick handwoven carpets covered the floor. We were ushered into a spacious room which was furnished in Western style with a long sofa and stuffed chairs. But the canopied bed, the rich carpet on the floor, and the silk draperies over the windows were all Chinese. The bed occupying half of the room was so huge I surmised the two of us would sleep in it.

Later in the afternoon, we hired two ponies and rode through the legendary city, stopping here and there to look in the shops. They were filled with displays of unusual crafts of forms in brass, bamboo, and porcelain. We saw on the distant hill a pagoda standing like a sentry. We rode out of town and galloped up the hill, dismounting at the foot of the old pagoda. That view of Soochow! The panorama of the ancient city spread out below us: a patchwork of farms and hamlets laced with dikes and footpaths. In their midst, an enormous lake mirrored reflections of old summer palaces. I looked up at the pagoda whose colors were all but faded and wondered about the scenes it must have witnessed when emperors with their retinue of musicians, dancers, and court ladies had come here to play and revel.

Back at the hotel we took a brief rest before dinner—an excellent fare in the elegant hotel restaurant. I dispelled my worries about the cost of such a lavish holiday, remembering that Chai came from a "very rich family." After dinner, we sat around the lounge to rest our heavy stomachs and make plans for the evening. It then occurred to me that beyond simple exchanges about food and prices, Chai and I had hardly talked to each other. Perhaps, being so many years apart, we didn't share anything of mutual interest. Besides, I thought, he was somewhat inarticulate, and his ever present grin did not inspire any conversation. So we just sat without a word, staring out the window. Finally, Chai broke the awkward silence.

"Pedro-Si," he still addressed me politely as though we were of equal status.

"Yes, Teacher Chai?" I, too, responded in polite form.

"Have you ever been with a girl?"

Startled, I looked around to see if anyone might be listening but then realized Chai was talking in Korean; no one could possibly know what we were talking about.

"I don't know what you mean . . . ," I said defensively even though I knew perfectly well what he meant.

"You know what I mean," he said, and with a wide grin Chai repeated, "Have you ever been with a girl?"

"Oh, that . . . ," I said nonchalantly. "Of course, many times. . . ."

"How many times?"

"Oh, I don't remember. . . ." I hoped he would drop the subject. I didn't want to keep lying to him, but neither did I want to tell him the truth that the only intimate contact I had ever had with a girl was when Luva, the girl from Russia, grabbed and kissed me, causing a battle royal in school.

"Well, in that case," Chai said, "how about having a girl tonight?"

I was totally unprepared for the proposal, but I was surprised to hear myself saying, "It's all right with me."

"Very good, Pedro-Si!" Chai slapped his knee and then confided, "I have arranged a separate room for you, and I'll send you a very pretty girl." He led me to a new room and left me there saying, "I'll see you in the morning, Pedro-Si."

I couldn't believe what was happening. Without being able to speak any Chinese, how did Chai manage to make such arrangements? Should I leave the room? Or should I stay? The situation was intriguing. In the legendary city of Soochow? Meet a legendary Soochow woman! The thoughts rushed through my head like wildfire. Soochow women had been known as the most beautiful in all China. Throughout history, emperors, generals, and ministers had come to Soochow for the explicit pleasure of the company of Soochow women, many of whom were taken away as concubines. And now, a Soochow woman would teach me how to be a man?

A knock at the door. I said "Yes?" and felt a little tremble in my voice. The door opened and a young woman tiptoed in shyly, smiling and greeting me in a soft, bubbling voice. At that moment, all sense of reality left me; I sank into a trance. I was aware of things around me, but it seemed as though I was watching someone else in a dream. I stood there helplessly and watched her undressing, quietly, slowly. Then, completely naked, she stood there for me to look and marvel at her young, shimmering body. It was my first sight of a naked woman. She was neither a girl nor a woman; she was an ethereal doll waiting to be touched and brought to life. But the entrancing sight was almost painful; I blinked and turned my eyes away.

Gently she pulled away the covers and slid into bed. She tilted her head and gazed at me with a warm, sweet smile. With her silent encouragement, I began to undress. I have no recollection of how I was able to shed all my clothes, my shoes and socks. I felt attacks of cold chills and hot flushes. But the watchful eyes of the living doll never left me and kept urging me to join her. I was lost.

With patience and understanding, she helped me slowly to lose my fright. She held my hand and guided me gently to touch and explore her. With every moment, the thrill and the excitement became more and more intense. She began making soft sounds of desire, but I didn't know how to respond. Understanding perfectly, she maneuvered herself and slid under me, while at the same time rolling me over her. Suddenly I lost all my fear; I was no longer helpless and passive. Oh, how simple yet how wonderful it was to be a man!

In the morning, I found Chai waiting for me in the lobby. His grin was bigger than ever.

"How was it?" he asked.

"Oh, all right," I answered with a newfound bravado. Actually, I felt sick—sick at having to share with someone else my first experience with a woman. But I could not ignore him; he was my benefactor. Perhaps I should thank him. Instead, I resented him and wished he would disappear.

"I want to go home," I said coldly.

"Why, Pedro-Si? We can spend a few days here."

"No, I want to go back," I insisted.

The train ride back to Shanghai was a silent one. I felt so resentful of Chai that he became repulsive to me. Back in Shanghai, I felt at home and safe. I was eager to be with my friends again: the Ahn boys, son and nephew of the Korean martyr; Park Hai-Yung, the joyous beauty from Russia; and, of course, the nearsighted genius Ok-Nyuh and all the rest. But when I met them, somehow my feelings were not the same; the innocent years of my youth seemed to have vanished. Overnight, it seemed, I had crossed the mystical chasm from boyhood to manhood, and all my youthful dreams suddenly assumed different dimensions. I was seventeen years old!

Father was still trudging around Manchuria selling English patent medicine. But his unflinching faith in his personal destiny was soon to be rewarded. He had covered the city of Mukden with posters, the city where he had begun his revolutionary activities for Korean independence. The next city was Chang-Choon. A letter was waiting for him there; it was from Dr. Fry, the Methodist superintendent in Hawaii, forwarded from Shanghai. Father read it to discover he was offered the pastorship of the Korean Methodist Church in Honolulu. The money for his travel was being sent, he was told, and eventually all his family could join him in Honolulu.

He resigned his salesman's job immediately to prepare for his trip to Hawaii. By taking the cheaper steerage class, he could take Sister Alice with him. On a chilly February evening in 1923, we all went to the wharf to bid Father and Sister Alice farewell. Someone carried my invalid sister Soon-Ok; she was thrilled to be out of doors and to see the inside of an oceangoing ship.

But how did Sister Alice happen to be accompanying Father to Hawaii? Her marriage to Chung quickly turned out to be a painful mistake. On the rich Chung family estate at the southern tip of Korea, she found herself relegated to the "women's quarters" while her husband spent his days with his friends in the "men's quarters." All the family wealth came from their tenant farmers, and they lived in the old feudal ways. Disheartened, Sister Alice tried to interest her husband in some useful activities in order not to waste his college education. Chung would not heed; he continued his life of an indolent landlord, immersed in the pleasures of drinking and playing.

Sister Alice gave birth to a baby girl, and as soon as she regained her strength, she let Chung know that she was leaving him. He didn't seem much concerned, but he wouldn't allow my sister to take her baby with her. It was not easy, but rather than holding onto her baby, she extricated herself and returned alone to Shanghai, hoping she could rebuild her damaged life. We were all elated to have her with us again. As for me, I felt I'd found my lost treasure. I had so much to confide to her and to ask her advice. Father too was happy to have Sister Alice accompany him to Hawaii. She could help him with his new church work, but even more important she could find a home for the day when Umma and the rest of the family would be joining them.

When, at last, our family seemed to be emerging out of the dark days, we faced the saddest of all tragedies. Sister Soon-Ok, my dearest sister and favorite playmate, became seriously ill and completely bedridden. When Umma took her to the City Hospital, they discovered that the long years of immobility had caused an internal infection which began to spread to vital organs. They told Umma that Soon-Ok had not much longer to live.

Umma and I visited her every other day. At each visit we could see the rapid wasting of her body. But Sister Soon-Ok was still vivacious and lively. During our visits, she had much to tell us: interesting stories about other patients and funny descriptions of the nurses to each of whom she had given a Korean nickname. From her bed, she observed everything happening around her. Telling her stories, she would forget her pain and laugh with us all through our visits.

One day, the visiting hours over, we said good-bye and began to leave the room. Suddenly Sister Soon-Ok called to us, and we went back to her bedside.

"Will you please come back tomorrow?" she whispered.

We were startled, for she had never begged any favors before. "Of course," Umma assured her, "we'll be back tomorrow."

When we went back the next day, she was already dead; they had already moved her body. Most of her eighteen years of life had been spent in bed in misery and pain. Now, finally, it all came to an end. With only a handful of friends present, we gave her a sad and lonely burial in a public cemetery on the outskirts of Shanghai.

14

NEW WORLD

Six months after his departure from China, Father sent us the first money to join him, but it wasn't enough for all of us to go to Hawaii. So, Umma decided that Sister Elizabeth and I should go first and take the two younger ones with us, Brother David and baby Sister Mary. Umma would remain in Shanghai with my brothers Paul and Joshua and wait for Father to send more money.

My first ocean voyage! We arrived at the Shanghai pier at dusk to find the docks crowded with people. All my friends—"the Little Revolutionaries"—were there to see us off. This would be the last time I would ever see or talk to them: Park Hai-Yung, the girl from Russia with large round eyes, and then of course Chai Ok-Nyuh, the nearsighted one who had such hidden feelings for me but was too shy to speak more than a few words at a time. When I was away in school in Nanking, she'd written to me faithfully. And there was Phillip Kim, the son of our foreign minister, and the Ahn boys, the son and the nephew of the great Korean patriot and martyr, Ahn Jung-Gun. What would become of all of them?

They stared at me enviously, and the shy one said, "You will soon become an American and forget us and forget Korea."

"Never," I cried. "I'll never forget you! And I'll never forget my motherland!"

Suddenly, bells began to ring loudly announcing the ship's departure, and all visitors had to get off the ship. The last words of my friends as they were leaving were, "Don't forget us! Don't forget us!"

NEW WORLD

Then Umma grasped my hand and gave me her final instructions. "Pedro-ya, listen to me. When the ship stops in Japan, don't get off the ship." I nodded. "Pedro-ya," Umma repeated, "promise me, Pedro-ya, you won't get off the ship. Remember, you can never trust the Japanese."

It was late at night when the ship slipped out of the dock and plowed through the muddy Whangpoo River, and finally into the open sea. Everything happening around me seemed strange and unreal. But strangest of all, I was sailing on a ship named SS *President Wilson*. It was President Wilson who had inspired the Korean people to revolt against the Japanese colonial rule, but when they did, that president turned his back and refused any help. And now, *President Wilson* was carrying the family of one of the leaders of the Korean uprising to his own homeland America!

It took two days to cross the Yellow Sea. I discovered why the sea was given such an ugly name; the entire ocean was a dirty brown mud color. On the morning of the third day, we entered Sedo-Nai-Kai, the Inland Sea of Japan. After floating on muddy water for two days, the crystal clear blue water of the Inland Sea was astonishing. From the ship's rail, I could look down and see the bottom of the ocean. On either side of the narrow strait, we could see the coastal land, and as we passed little islands shaded by clusters of pine trees, we could see tiny thatched-roof houses, fishnets hung out and drying, and women washing clothes at the water's edge. Thin streams of smoke rose here and there signaling that the families of the fishermen were busy preparing breakfast.

Sister Elizabeth and I were fascinated to see parts of the world shaped so differently and populated by people with their own special way of life. The wondrous Inland Sea was very long; it took the whole day to pass through. Then the ship sailed onto the Pacific Ocean. This, I had learned in school, was the largest body of water in the world, and I was sailing on it. This great ocean not only protected the American mainland but also the major islands of Japan: Kyushu, Shikoku, Honshu, and Hokkaido.

The first Japanese port we reached was Kobe. The ship docked to remain there overnight. Sister Elizabeth, holding onto baby Sister Mary, and I, holding onto Brother David, leaned against the rail watching all the activities on the pier. All the people were Japanese, of course, and this was their homeland. For the first time I was looking at my enemies in their own land. I saw passengers going ashore for sight-seeing expeditions. Umma's final instructions were still fresh in my mind, but the temptation to set my feet down and walk around "Ene-myland" was irresistible.

Just then, two American men approached and invited me to join them and go ashore. Oh, how I would have liked to do that, but I had to tell them, "No, I can't. I am a Korean and I could be arrested by the Japanese."

"Nonsense," they said, "you come with us. We are Americans . . . we'll protect you."

I turned to Sister Elizabeth and asked, "What do you think?"

"It's up to you," she replied.

"All right," I said to the American, "I go."

These two men were not like the Americans I used to see in Shanghai, haughty and arrogant. They were traveling in the steerage just like us. Later, I found out from bits of stories they told me that they had come to Shanghai as stowaways. They had no money, so they went to the American consulate for help. The officials decided that their tramplike appearance would disgrace the Americans in Shanghai, and put them on the SS *President Wilson* (steerage class) to ship them back to America. At the time, the story sounded too strange for me to understand; they looked like Americans, they talked like Americans.

They were delighted to hear me say, "All right, I go." Each hold-ing my arm, they led me down the gangplank, and I stepped on the land of the Rising Sun. At that moment, I heard again Umma's last warning, "You can never trust the Japanese. . . ." I became quite tense, and carefully noted the streets and plotted in my mind how to escape should the Japanese police try to arrest me. The two Americans laughed and patted me saying, "Don't be nervous . . . nothing can happen to you . . . you are with us . . . Americans."

Somewhat relieved, I became more absorbed by the strange sur-roundings. Both sides of the narrow street were lined with low, box-like wooden houses with black tile roofs. Only the occasional two-story buildings broke the symmetrical pattern. And except for the glass windows of shops, all the houses had paper windows with wooden lattices. Crowds of people in colorful clothes, especially women and children, sauntered along the street. Quite a few of them were wearing *geta*—wooden slippers—whose clatter on the street sounded like noisy insects in the forest at night.

The whole town seemed to be celebrating some kind of festival. Decorations made of paper, pine twigs, and ribbons hung everywhere: on the eaves, windows, and doors and on long bamboo poles. Paper lanterns of bright colors hung across the street row on row and swayed gently in the evening breeze. We followed the crowd and came to a little park where the festivity seemed to be centered. The entire park was encircled with lanterns of all colors and shapes, and more decorations hung on every tree.

In the center of the park, a miniature temple stood on a high platform. Musicians could be seen sitting on the temple floor singing to the beat of a large drum. Around the temple, men, women, and children danced in a circle. In unison, they clapped, stepped back and forth, and spun themselves around. As they repeated the movements, the dancers joined the musicians in singing the chantlike song. Shouts of *"Joi! Joi!"*—equivalent to *"Hao! Hao!"* in China—rang out from the crowd watching the dancing. Everyone laughed, clapped, and kept time with the dancers. I was completely overcome by the sight; I had never seen any Japanese people laughing, not to mention singing and dancing. In Korea, I had known them only as a grim and cruel people whose only skills, I believed, were scheming, robbing, and killing.

We traced our way back to the ship. On the way, I stopped at a pastry shop and bought some *mochi*—Japanese cake which I could only stare at through the window in Seoul, never having the money to buy and taste. When we came aboard, Sister Elizabeth rushed to me almost in tears; she had been desperately worried that something dreadful had happened to me. I pushed my chest out and showed Sister Elizabeth how unafraid I had been. The two Americans watched and understood my pantomime and broke into a hearty laugh. Then to comfort Elizabeth and the little ones, I offered them the bag of *mochi*. They ate them but without much relish.

That night, before going to sleep in the dark steerage hold, I thought of those Japanese people singing and dancing; they seemed such happy, ordinary people. And all my life I had hated them. Indeed, only recently I had thought of joining the Korean guerrillas in Manchuria so that I could kill all the Japanese I could find.

Another day of sailing brought us to Yokohama, the largest Japanese seaport, and only an hour's train ride from Tokyo. The ship was to remain in the harbor overnight, so there was ample time to visit Japan's capital. Oh, what a temptation! And the two Americans were once more urging me to come with them. But I decided not to leave the ship again; it would be too cruel to subject Sister Elizabeth and the little ones to another time of fear and worry over me. Instead I contented myself leaning over the railing, scanning the view of the city in the distance and watching the Japanese workmen scurrying about carrying heavy loads in and out of the ship.

At dawn, we saw the last of the harbor and Japan. We sailed for ten days and nights without seeing anything but water; not even another ship. I passed the time mostly by visiting other steerage passengers, Chinese and Japanese but no other Koreans. I was anxious to find out where they all came from and where they were going. To my surprise, most of the Chinese came not from China but from such outlying countries as the Philippines, Hong Kong, Indochina, and as far as India. It was the first inkling I had of the vast spread of Chinese people around the world. The Japanese passengers always remained isolated in their own circle. When I approached them, they seemed suspicious and were reluctant to talk or reveal any of their background, even though I spoke to them in Japanese. Though reticent, however, they were always extremely polite. I did succeed in discovering that all the Chinese and the Japanese immigrants were going to the American mainland: San Francisco, Los Angeles. They all had friends or relatives waiting for them. I was quite envious.

Compared to such "tooth-pulling" visits with fellow Orientals, it was more fruitful and fun to visit with the two Americans. They were quite open and friendly and answered all my questions. It was a wonderful chance for me to practice my meager English and to learn many new words and expressions such as "no kidding," "O.K.," "what's the matter?" and "I'm with you." But the part of my visit with them that I enjoyed most were my eager questions about America: Were there streets really paved with gold? Are all Americans faithful Christians? Do all American boys and girls go to college? What kind of houses do they live in, and how many times a day do they eat? And so on and so on without end. . . .

Throughout the long voyage, we had to suffer through the ordeal of being fed—three times a day. Each meal was exactly like all the others. Two seamen hauled down a large tub and set it down on the filthy steerage floor, and each passenger was handed a metal bowl and a spoon. The age-old dirt on the floor and the ever-present sour stench in the hold were not conducive to stirring anyone's appetite. Just the same, everyone stood in line and took turns scooping the food out of the tub. For our little ones, Sister Elizabeth had to do the scooping for them. The food was invariably the same: a tasteless thick soup. But without exception, everybody ate his fill to make sure not to get hungry before the next meal.

Another daily ordeal was the ritual of going to sleep. All the steerage passengers slept in narrow canvas bunks suspended on metal posts in two tiers. First I would toss Brother David up to the top bunk and cover him with a coarse blanket. Then I would help Sister Elizabeth settle baby Sister Mary in a lower bunk, and help her climb into the top one. I could then roll into my own lower bunk and prepare myself to go to sleep. After the first few hectic nights, we became expert steerage dwellers. We also became seasoned sailors. Even little David and baby Sister Mary moved about the ship without lurching or staggering backwards.

On the morning of the fifteenth day, I was awakened by an excited commotion on deck. I got up hastily and went up to find the people pointing and yelling, "Look! Look! Look!" I could see a faint outline of land on the horizon. After fourteen days of floating on water with nothing in sight, it was a miracle to see land looming out of the sea.

At that moment, for no apparent reason, I remembered our family's first exodus—the desolate journey across the Manchurian desert. It was so long ago; baby Sister Mary was not quite one, Brother David was three years old, Sister Elizabeth, fifteen, and I, fourteen. All of us, even Umma, were in utter bewilderment. We were traveling farther and farther away from Korea, but no one knew what kind of world and what kind of life we were plunging into. We were only content to be escaping from the Japanese; life anywhere would be better than living under the heel of the Japanese police.

And now we were on our second exodus, even farther away from our home in Korea and away from our home in China. But for some reason, the filth and the stench of traveling in steerage did not make us feel desolate and lost. On the contrary, we were sustained and buoyed by new visions. We were being carried to a new and better world. This was a happy journey filled with endless hopes and exciting dreams.

As the ship sailed closer, the island grew bigger and bigger until we could see the strange symmetrical ridges arising from the sea straight up to the top of the mountain. They looked like the giant ribs of a prehistoric monster. But when the ship circled the island, the jagged rocks melted into luscious tropical forests and verdant valleys with palm trees lining the shores. I had only read about palm fronds in the Bible, but there before my eyes were the living coconut and royal palms swaying and waving in the breeze.

Was this really the Promised Land? Was it the Island Paradise? There, beyond the rocks and the palm trees, would I find the New World where all the promises and dreams would be fulfilled? It was May 1924; I was seventeen years old.

PHOTOGRAPHS

Peter dolled up for Sister Alice's wedding in Shanghai in 1922.

Peter, 1924

Brother Joshua, 1925

Sister Alice, 1923

Brother Paul, ca. 1930

Brother David, in the 1930s

Baby Sister Mary, in the 1930s

Soon Hyun (left) about 1895 as a student of the Royal English Academy, the first Western school established by the last king of Korea.

The young patriot Soon Hyun (standing, right) with his colleagues.

The Korean Commission to America and Europe, created by the Korean Provisional Government in Shanghai. From left: Henry Chung, Kim Kiu-Sik, and Soon Hyun.

The Reverend Soon Hyun, 1921.

Maria Hyun, 1924

Maria Hyun in 1950

Soon Hyun and Maria Hyun with their first granddaughter,
Ruth, and grandson Paul.

ABOUT THE AUTHOR

Peter Hyun was born in Hawaii in 1906 but grew up in Seoul, Korea, where his father, the Reverend Soon Hyun, was one of the leaders of the Korean independence movement struggling against Japanese colonial rule. A year after the March First uprising in 1919, in which Peter participated, the family escaped to Shanghai to join Reverend Hyun, who with other Korean patriots had established the independent Korean Provisional Government in Exile. When Peter was seventeen, the family moved to Hawaii, where Peter graduated from Kauai High School. After attending DePauw University in Indiana, where he majored in philosophy and theatre arts, he plunged into professional work in the American theatre. He was stage manager for Eva LeGallienne's Civic Repertory Theatre in New York, director of the Children's Theatre of the New York Federal Theatre, and the organizer and director of the Studio Players in Cambridge, Massachusetts. In World War II he served as a language specialist in the U.S. Army in the Pacific theatre. After several business ventures, he settled in Oxnard, California, and taught English as a Second Language to immigrant students from Asia—Thailand, Vietnam, China, Korea, and Japan. He is now retired and writing full time.

⬚ Production Notes

This book was designed by Roger Eggers. Composition and paging were done on the Quadex Composing System and typesetting on the Compugraphic 8400 by the design and production staff of University of Hawaii Press.

The text and display typeface is Compugraphic Bembo.

Offset presswork and binding were done by Vail-Ballou Press, Inc. Text paper is Glatfelter Offset Vellum, basis 50.